WHAT TO DO IN RETIREMENT

Aaron Tellers

Copyright © 2020 Aaron Tellers

All rights reserved.

ISBN: 9798627397375

WHAT TO DO IN *RETIREMENT*

Disclaimer: The contents of this book are for general information purposes only. Neither the publisher nor author shall be held liable for any loss or damages to the reader resulting from the information contained herein.

WARNING!

This book is not entirely factually accurate. It contains some thoroughly bad advice and may cause injury or death if taken too seriously. Some of the activities described herein may be fun to talk about but are decidedly unfun to do! Proceed with caution, you have been warned!

Contents

ACKNOWLEDGMENTS 1
1 INTRODUCTION 2
2 ARTISTIC 10
3 CRAFTY 17
4 HEAD TO YOUR SHED 25
5 THE GREAT OUTDOORS 29
6 SOCIAL 34
7 GOING SOLO 39
8 MUSICAL 41
9 LITERARY 45
10 EDUCATIONAL 49
11 POLITICAL 52
12 VOYEURISTIC 54
13 PERFORMING 58
14 HEDONISTIC 63
15 SPORTY 67
16 LUCRATIVE 76
17 SPIRITUAL 81
18 CHARITABLE 84
19 NOMADIC 87
20 THE LIFE AQUATIC 91
21 TECHNICAL 94
22 FAMILY ORIENTED 96
23 A Quick Word In Closing 98
Resources 99

WHAT TO DO IN *RETIREMENT*

ACKNOWLEDGMENTS

Welcome to retirement! Congratulations on making it over the all the hurdles and reaching that wonderful time of life where you get to do whatever you want. No more morning commute, no more idiotic bosses, no more stressful deadlines! You are now officially off the clock and the world is your oyster! While it may seem easy to just settle back and continue doing the things we have always done, why not mix it up a bit, break the inertia and get out and try something new? What have you got to lose?

There is no need to be bound by convention, push the envelope, do it weird, do it different, but most of all do it fun! Be that cigar chomping rock'n'roll granny if it takes your fancy. Seriously, if your kids aren't worried about what you are up to, then you are probably not doing it right!

When I set out to write this book my aim was to crack open the unexplored world and have a look at what there is out there. It was never my intention to give excessively detailed instructions on any given suggestion, (and I think I have pretty well succeeded on that count), nor was it my intention to offer a load of patronizing advice on how to manage your finances, eat healthily or stay fit. (I am fairly certain that no one wants or needs my opinion on how they aught to manage their life). That said, there is an exciting world of possibilities out there that very few of us get the chance to explore during our working lives, but retirement is that time! The following pages contain far more than the promised 101 suggestions, so if you find some of them a bit lame or not quite to your taste feel free to view them as a unwanted bonus gifts (not unlike those free steak knifes that come with every product ever sold on TV), and enjoy the rest.

On a personal note: Before you start reading I have a bit of a confession to make. When I sat down to write this book I had every intention of writing a totally 'straight' book with nothing too weird or wacky in it, but as is often the way with me things pretty soon ran off the rails. In spite of my best efforts to keep my quirky in check it kept leaking out onto the page. In the end I decided to just go with it and I added the subtitle. As a result what initially began as a fairly normal book gets intermittently weirder as it goes along. While it starts out in a reasonably conventional fashion it soon starts to get a bit strange. I pulled it all back into line several times and of course, me being me, it just kept getting weird again. At first this bothered me, I had no idea how I was going to finish the book if I tried to take all my peculiarities out, but once I freed myself from the shackles of expectation I began to really enjoy the mix of the two, so I decided to leave it that way. I hope the mix works you too. After all, retirement is all about having the freedom to do it the way you want to, so I did. I sincerely hope you enjoy!

1 INTRODUCTION

Welcome to retirement! Congratulations on making it over the all the hurdles and reaching that wonderful time of life where you get to do whatever you want. No more morning commute, no more idiotic bosses, no more stressful deadlines! You are now officially off the clock and the world is your oyster! While it may seem easy to just settle back and continue doing the things we

WHAT TO DO IN *RETIREMENT*

have always done, why not mix it up a bit, break the inertia and get out and try something new? What have you got to lose?

There is no need to be bound by convention, push the envelope, do it weird, do it different, but most of all do it fun! Be that cigar chomping rock'n'roll granny if it takes your fancy. Seriously, if your kids aren't worried about what you are up to, then you are probably not doing it right!

When I set out to write this book my aim was to crack open the unexplored world and have a look at what there is out there. It was never my intention to give excessively detailed instructions on any given suggestion, (and I think I have pretty well succeeded on that count), nor was it my intention to offer a load of patronizing advice on how to manage your finances, eat healthily or stay fit. (I am fairly certain that no one wants or needs my opinion on how they aught to manage their life). That said, there is an exciting world of possibilities out there that very few of us get the chance to explore during our working lives, but retirement is that time! The following pages contain far more than the promised 101 suggestions, so if you find some of them a bit lame or not quite to your taste feel free to view them as a unwanted bonus gifts (not unlike those free steak knifes that come with every product ever sold on TV), and enjoy the rest.

On a personal note: Before you start reading I have a bit of a confession to make. When I sat down to write this book I had every intention of writing a totally 'straight' book with nothing too weird or wacky in it, but as is often the way with me things pretty soon ran off the rails. In spite of my best efforts to keep my quirky in check it kept leaking out onto the page. In the end I decided to just go with it and I added the subtitle. As a result what initially began as a fairly normal book gets intermittently weirder as it goes along. While it starts out in a reasonably conventional fashion it soon starts to get a bit strange. I pulled it all back into line several times and of course, me being me, it just kept getting weird again. At first this bothered me, I had no idea how I was going to finish the book if I tried to take all my peculiarities out, but once I freed myself from the shackles of expectation I began to really enjoy the mix of the two, so I decided to leave it that way. I hope the mix works you too. After all, retirement is all about having the freedom to do it the way you want to, so I did. I sincerely hope you enjoy!

What Is Retirement?

WHAT TO DO IN *RETIREMENT*

English is a notoriously difficult language. As the bastard son of the Latin, Nordic and Teutonic language groups, it has so many homonyms and synonyms that trying to accurately define the meaning of anything can be enough to make your brain bleed. Given English's linguistic latitude it should come as no surprise that the word 'retirement' has many variations in meaning, each with its own shades, colours and overtones, and that any definition is going to be subject to interpretation. So, when seeking to understand what is meant by retirement, the first stop is quite naturally the dictionary.

www.dictionary.com describes retirement thus:

1. The act of retiring, withdrawing, or leaving; the state of being retired.

2. The act of retiring or of leaving one's job, career, or occupation permanently, usually because of age: "I'm looking forward to my retirement from teaching".

3. The portion of a person's life during which a person is retired: "What will you do in retirement?"

4. Removal of something from service or use: Retirement of the space shuttle fleet.

5. Withdrawal of a jury from a courtroom to deliberate in private on a verdict.

6. Orderly withdrawal of a military force, according to plan, without pressure from the enemy.

Personally, I am not at all satisfied with these definitions. With the best will in the world they have failed to capture the dramatic and exciting nature of the occasion! All this 'leaving' and 'withdrawing' is pretty damn dour; and choosing to frame one's retirement in such terms could be a tad depressing. So, in the joyous spirit of reinvention I would like to propose a bit of a rewrite.

1.The act of retiring, withdrawing, or leaving; the state of being retired.

Really, this definition is quite awful, and totally backward looking! The fact is you cannot 'withdraw from' or 'leave' one place without moving to another, so why put all the focus on the leaving? Why not put a little more emphasis on where you are going? It could just as easily read something like this:

WHAT TO DO IN *RETIREMENT*

1. The act of retiring, entering a new self-determined phase of life, leaving the employ or oversight of others to exercise greater choice and freedom in the use of one's time; the state of being retired.

How much better is that? Who wouldn't want to "exercise greater choice and freedom in the use of ones time"? It's like a lottery win.

---

2. The act of retiring or of leaving one's job, career, or occupation permanently, usually because of age: "I'm looking forward to my retirement from teaching."

This one is troublesome in a number of ways, as it suggests that one is leaving one's "career or occupation permanently". Naturally if one is leaving a job they hate then popping the cork on the bubbly is entirely appropriate; but if you have a career or occupation that you love, one might not feel so inclined to celebrate, particularly if the choice to retire was not entirely your own. However, all is not lost. In almost every field imaginable there are options to continue your beloved life's work in some form or another. Teachers can become private tutors and mentors. Hairdressers can have clients call by the house. Stockbrokers can still trade on the Internet. Many retired builders give great service in hardware stores. Your lifetime of skills and knowledge is of great value and there is absolutely no reason to set it aside if you don't want to. This definition could just as rightly read:

2. The act of retiring, to permanently leave one's job, career, or occupation: or to reduce or restructure one's level of workplace involvement to better suit one's changing desires and capacities, after many years of work: "I'm looking forward to my retirement from teaching, and taking up part time tutoring".

After all retirement doesn't mean stopping dead in ones tracks, (unless of course you want to).

OK, this next one is dead easy.

3. The portion of a person's life during which a person is retired: "What will you do in retirement?"

Becomes:

3. The portion of a person's life during which one's activity is totally self-

WHAT TO DO IN *RETIREMENT*

determined, and one is no longer required to work for a living: "What will you do in retirement?"

A much happier option I think!

4. Removal of something from service or use: Retirement of the space shuttle fleet.

This is more or less OK as it is, although in this context the word removal has a bit of a harsh overtone. It would seem like much more fun if it read:

4. Removing the burden of 'service or use" imposed on a person or object by forces beyond their control. Retirement of the space shuttle fleet. (At last the poor thing can finally relax, all that launching and re-entering can really take a toll).

5. Withdrawal of a jury from a courtroom to deliberate in private on a verdict.

This one I actually like, as it is one of the few definitions that is proactive. That jury is off to do something important. They are going to apply their minds, utilise their critical faculties and exercise moral judgement. This is the kind of retirement that I can relate to!

6. Orderly withdrawal of a military force, according to plan, without pressure from the enemy.

This is probably the best definition of the lot. What could be better than the ceasing of hostilities and the withdrawal of troops? Imagine a world where we could retire all the armies, now that would really be something.

OK, now that we have some more upbeat interpretations of what retirement actually is, it's time to give some thought as to how you would like to define your retirement.

Sea Change Or Tree Change?

I'm going to keep this short. Are you in the right place? Do you need to move somewhere more suitable to your interests, physical needs or budget? If so,

WHAT TO DO IN *RETIREMENT*

this is the first thing you should attend to. If you are going to create a new life for yourself then you need to get the foundation right. No point in investing vast amounts of energy building a network of new friends and location specific activities if you are going to up stumps and move in six months.

Carpe Diem, I say! If you are going to do the change, best get on with it!

What About The Finances?

No one needs a lot of money. Having lived most my life as a freelancer working in the arts, I can say this with a good deal of authority! Creativity, curiosity, kindness and a sense of adventure will make you happier and bring you more genuine friends than any amount of money in the bank. If you have money, that's great. However, if you don't have much money then life has issued you a challenge, but it is a challenge you can meet! Most creative endeavours don't require a lot of cash. If your financial circumstances dictate that you must choose from inexpensive options just remember, your imagination has no such limitations. Your novel can be just as epic as the novel written by a millionaire! Your picnic can be just as wonderful as a dinner at a celebrity-studded restaurant. Think outside the box, you will be amazed at all the possibilities lurking out there!

What Kind Of Retirement?

No matter what age we are, there are certain things that everyone requires in order to feel happy and fulfilled. We all need the friendship, love and companionship of like-minded people. We all need healthy food, fresh air and clean water. We all need time to ourselves to reflect. We all need to challenge ourselves and push our boundaries, and last, but by no means least, we all need a sense of purpose. Unfortunately for many people, one or more of these things often falls by the wayside when we are mired in the daily grind of work, mortgage and small children. All too often life rushes by and somehow we end up at the end of our working lives feeling like we have missed our calling. Fortunately we now live in an age where most of us can expect two, three, maybe even four decades of reasonably good health in retirement, in which we can live true to our own sense of purpose. For some people retirement can span well over half their adult life, so the last thing you'd want to do is waste it! Human life is so precious, and having been granted such a gift there really is no excuse for not getting out there and doing whatever it is

WHAT TO DO IN *RETIREMENT*

that makes you happy!

No matter what your finances, inclinations or capacity, the world is overflowing with possibilities. Not only have we been blessed with extraordinary minds, we have been given dexterous hands (with opposable thumbs), complex language, and a strong desire to better ourselves. Whatever else we may be, we humans are fundamentally goal oriented, achievement driven beings that thrive on challenge and purpose, and that doesn't change just because we hit retirement.

So, now that you are free to go wherever and do whatever you like, what is it that you actually want to do? How on earth do you choose? There are so many incredible options it can be difficult to narrow it down. Most of us have an inclination towards particular interests and activities, but few of us have explored all the possibilities available within those spheres. If, for example, you have dreamed of spending your retirement cruising the Bahamas on your hundred-foot yacht but your finances don't look like they will stretch that far, do not despair. If you think laterally you may find your favourite activities can be done on a shoestring; or you can devise a plan B from the extraordinary range of activities that cost little or no money at all. Whatever your dreams you don't need millions. The world is stuffed stupid with fun and rewarding things to do and you now have the luxury of time and choice.

Of course, what ever you do you will need to prioritize. Anything that requires robust health, like that trek up Everest, is probably something you should do sooner rather than later, whereas reading the complete works of Dostoevsky could possibly wait a bit. But what ever your health, budget or life circumstances, there is a full and wonderful life to be lived. There are flavours to taste, flowers to smell, songs to be sung and boundless joy to be had. Your life is now 100% YOURS, and it is really only just beginning! You now have the reigns firmly in your hands, so get out there and live it LARGE!

To make this book easier to navigate I have sorted it into the broad categories of arty, crafty, literary, political, social, educational, hedonistic, the great outdoors, performing, voyeuristic, charitable, family oriented, nomadic, musical, sporty, spiritual, technical and the life aquatic. I suggest you read them all though, as you may find quite a number of things that pique your interest listed in sections that you would have never previously considered.

WHAT TO DO IN *RETIREMENT*

WHAT TO DO IN *RETIREMENT*

2 ARTISTIC

Many people have dreamed of living an artistic life, only to find the practical demands of the world have proved too great an obstacle. When one is working full time there can be little energy left at the end of the day for artistic endeavours, but now you have your freedom you can let your artistic side run wild. You may unleash a powerfully weird talent that has been lurking deep inside just waiting for its chance to emerge. Whether you are tossing aside convention and conjuring up abstract images of pure imagination, or interpreting a carefully staged still life, creating something from nothing is one of this world's most satisfying experiences. There is boundless joy, beauty and freedom to be found in the visual arts.

Arts and crafts can be amazingly social too; there are all kinds of groups, classes, and societies where people share tips and tricks, and bitch about each other's work. There are even groups that get together to contribute to larger works. Kids also love getting messy with arts and crafts, so what better way to engage your grand-kids than to get their best clothes covered in paint and glitter before you send them back home?

Picture This

Whether you choose to paint, draw, sketch or print, in our post-modern world NO RULES apply! You can throw paint, scratch, scrawl, drip, smear, daub, do what ever takes your fancy. There are literally thousands of online courses, groups and classes you can explore. Most cities have a favourite spot where artists tend to gather on sunny a day, so why not dig out your easel and get out there and join them. There are also countless opportunities to exhibit your work; from galleries to local coffee shops, everyone wants art! If a picture paints a thousand words, why not have your say?

WHAT TO DO IN *RETIREMENT*

Painting

Personally I love throwing paint around. I put everything into my abstracts; old train or theatre tickets, coins, newspaper, I even use cheap acrylic gap filler for an impasto medium. (Impasto is a thick textured layer in an artwork). There's no need to go to the expense of investing in professional paints. If you are simply a pleasure-seeking dabbler on a budget you could try creating with watercolours, aquarelles (watercolour pencil) or acrylic paints. You can get going for next to nothing. The old house paint stashed in the garage will do just fine to start with. Local discount stores are awash with inexpensive art supplies that are perfectly fine. I used our old sample pots with a kid's brush sets and cheap dime store canvasses to make stunning artworks for my house. I even sold a few paintings!

But really you don't even need paper or canvases; you can paint on an old sheet, a piece of Masonite, or even a cardboard box. Of course if you are drawn to something a bit more refined you can always build up a collection of quality art materials over time, but it's certainly not necessary to get you started. All you need is imagination and bravery and you are on your way.

Drawing

Why not check out a life drawing class. You don't need pricey brushes or expensive paints, all you need is a piece of charcoal and you are up and running. If you are on a tight budget then drawing with pencils, or even cartooning with felt pens and coloured ink, are delightfully inexpensive ways of getting an image onto paper. However, if you fancy your self as a potential Picasso (and you're not afraid of the cost), you might even want to try some of the more expensive forms such as quality coloured pencils, Conte crayons or soft pastels.

Printmaking

Printmaking has been steadily growing in popularity ever since Gutenberg pulled the first print off his revolutionary press. Of course, printing a book or magazine is not the same as making art, but the fundamental principals have been well adapted to the cause. Whether you choose one of the more demanding "high art" methods, such as screen-printing or lithograph, or one of your kitchen table varieties like potato or linoleum cut, printmaking is a truly beautiful art form. If you don't have a lot of cash to splash you could simply get together with the grand-kids and stamp cheap acrylic paints onto calico or butcher's paper with hand carved potato cuts. But if you want to go a bit more high end there plenty of classes and studios out there where you can learn to etch copper plates or make silk screens, and more importantly get your hands on the necessary equipment.

Collage

Cut out, juxtapose and stick down, these are the three commandments of collage. As an art form, collage is especially good for social commentary. Many contemporary news and science magazines make great fodder for keen the social commentator. Collage has also moved into the digital age. This is most clearly on display in the proliferation of online memes. In fact, some creative type is probably busy right now cutting and pasting Donald Trump's head onto the body of a chicken, and emblazoning it with some pithy remark. You can, of course, just get decorative with the form, but there are so many outrageous images out there, both printed and digital; it's hard to resist the temptation to get a little bit political.

Become An Art Critic

While technically not art in itself, becoming and art critic is a great way to get involved in the arts without having to have any special artistic skills or talents. After all, art is all about the attitude and the expression. In the art word the execution of an idea is never as important as impressing random cravat wearing people with your inscrutable, multi-syllabic art-speak. Playing art critic is loads of fun. Most people will be completely baffled by what you are saying, but will still stroke their chins thoughtfully, nod in agreement and throw back another red wine.

However, if you are having a bit of trouble coming up with the necessary inane art-speak to make your commentary seem deep and important enough, don't worry. As always the Internet has the solution. Introducing the "arty bollocks generator".

http://www.artybollocks.com/

The arty bollocks generator invites you to "Generate your own artist statement for free, and if you don't like it, generate another one. Feel free to

WHAT TO DO IN *RETIREMENT*

use the statements with funding applications, exhibitions, curriculum vitae, websites etc."

Example: "This work comments on the deconstruction of structuralism. It's about humanity's existential struggle for a segregated autonomy within in the post isolationist miasma that is an inherent feature of life within the critical density of mass urban colonization"

Instant critic! How good is that?

Get Into "Street Art"

Depending on where you live, street art is either considered graffiti or a revered art form that enhances amenity and social inclusion. But whatever it is, it is not just for teenagers. Many cities have places where street art is encouraged. If you are lucky enough to live in one of those places, why not get out there and make your mark. If not talk to the local authorities and see if you can get a designated "art space" going. When done in a properly allocated space, street art provides a fantastic forum for cross-generational communication and community engagement. As a case in point, in a city near me the local authority turned over an abandoned factory to street artists, and it now draws huge crowds of tourists every weekend.

Snap Into Photography

Whether it is a candid snap or staged masterpiece, photography is an art form. With the click of button a photograph distils the essence of a moment, reflecting the deeper truths of our existence. A photograph can shift perceptions, alter our constructs of reality and reveal untold stories that have the power to profoundly change our lives. *(See that arty bollocks really does come in handy)*.

All bollocks aside, you don't need to have a top-notch kit to catch a moment in your lens. If you have a half way decent camera on your phone it's more than good enough to start with; and there are a huge range of stunning filters and effects available on apps like Instagram and Hipstermatic that you can download to your phone for free. There is also an ever-growing collection of inexpensive lenses for under $50 that you can clip onto your smart phone camera for a more professional result. If budget is a concern then using your smart phone to shoot spontaneous, un-staged subject matter, (such as urban

WHAT TO DO IN *RETIREMENT*

photography or nature photography) is an excellent way to go.

However, if you would prefer to get your self a decent SLR camera it's good to know they have never been more affordable. And of course, digital photography means no more film or processing, so once you have the camera you can keep on shooting with no additional outlay.

If you are reasonably computer savvy there are wonderful photo editing programs like GIMP that are available for free (and loads of YouTube tutorials available to teach you how to use them), so you don't have to outlay thousands to use top notch programs like Adobe Photoshop, (although you can now subscribe to adobe's complete range of drawing, layout and photo editing software for a small monthly fee, so it could be worth signing up for a month or two to see if it is for you).

Once you have a portfolio of works you could mount an exhibition. There are plenty of inexpensive, good looking, "art" frames available at places like IKEA and you can get high quality prints done at your local print centre. Alternately, you could start an online gallery, set up a web site, or offer your shots for download on a "stock image" site*. There are also lot's of places like "www.shutterfly.com" where you can have your shots printed on a canvas, T-shirt or coffee mug, or assembled into a high quality printed book or calendar. What better way to make personalised gifts for your family and friends?

*(Offering your photos for sale on stock image sites can bring in a fair bit of cash if your shots prove to be popular. I recommend you try "www.bigstock.com" It's a popular choice for amateur and professional photographers alike.)

Sculpt Another Reality

With extraordinary works like Salvador Dali's giant poo covered building to Jeff Comb's "puppy", sculpture is now officially out of the box. You can make practically anything. Make a moo fish, a winged cat or a gigantic eyeball on a stick. No matter what the medium, the limit is your imagination. You don't have to do expensive bronze cast statues or chisel marble like Michelangelo; all kinds of everyday household junk can be turned into sculptural masterpieces. Clay, papier-mâché, chicken wire, plaster of Paris,

WHAT TO DO IN *RETIREMENT*

old toilet roll centres, railway sleepers, used drink bottles, wax, cd's, dead bicycles, old TVs, rusting farm equipment, anything can be turned into a sculpture.

I am currently building a sculptural "Birth of the robot Venus/Medusa" out of an old clam shaped toddler pool, a mannequin and some old ipads, TV's, cell phones and bag of old toy snakes for the hair. *(Although to be honest, I'm not at all sure what I am going to do with it, once it's finished).*

I admit there are some sculptural some forms, like welding or fibreglass, that require a fair bit of cash and an excess of shed space, but there are plenty of smaller projects that are inexpensive, not quite so space hungry and relatively easy to do. For example, carving aerated concrete blocks is particularly good for making garden sculptures. Aerated concrete is readily available in a range of sizes at most building suppliers. It is remarkably inexpensive, lightweight and can even be chiselled with a butter knife. What's more, it looks totally stunning, it's extremely easy to work with and you can achieve some very impressive results without too much practice or skill. With aerated concrete you could turn your garden into a miniature sculpture park with very little effort.

If you need a little more inspiration try Googling up images of "Sculpture by the sea" (which is the world's largest annual sculpture exhibition), and check out some of the amazing works.

Become An Artists Model

If you like the fine arts and enjoy the company of artists, but really don't feel like creating your own; why not get a gig as an artist's model? If the idea of being paid to sit around with your kit off floats your boat then this one is definitely for you. It's one of the very few activities you can do naked where the older (and less conventionally perfect) your body is, the more they love you. Bumps, rolls, cellulite and pot-bellies; artists just adore them. After all, the more unique your body, the more interesting and challenging you are to draw. The money isn't bad either!

WHAT TO DO IN *RETIREMENT*

3 CRAFTY

If the idea of doing "high art" doesn't appeal you might fancy directing your creative drive into something a little more practical. For centuries artisans have used their imagination, their sense of design and their manual skills to make all kinds of beautiful, practical things that serve humanity.

Pottery

Slick and slippery, oozing ones fingers through slimy clay on a potters wheel is pure magic. Hand-crafted pottery pieces are not only unique; they can also be extremely useful. Stunning hand painted plates, platters and bowls grace many of the finest tables.

Potters clay is inexpensive and easily obtained from your local arts supply. If you do not have a potter's wheel or a kiln there are lots studios and classes where you can try your hand; or you could simply start with a lump of clay and try hand shaping the object of your desire. For those that don't have access to a kiln there are "self-hardening" or "air dried" clays available on the market; I even heard of someone baking their clay in the microwave. As for the glazing side of things, as long as it is not being used for the dining table you can simply paint and seal your creation with regular house paint and a good strong polyurethane. There are also a number of different coloured modelling clays, such as "Fimo" or "Das" available that you can bake in the oven to harden. These products are wonderful for finer work like jewellery making. From pendants, earrings and bracelets to fruit bowls and garden pots, there is no limit to what you can make.

Sew What?

You will be relieved to know that the days of making lace tissue box covers are officially over. Today you can design and make absolutely anything, and

WHAT TO DO IN *RETIREMENT*

the wilder the better! Make yourself a hat, a coat, a dress, or a pair of rabbit ears. You could make fancy dress costumes for Halloween, or an Edwardian gown for a cross dresser.

If you are not up for designing something from scratch many charity shops have boxes full of old paper patterns that you can adapt to suit your imagination. My mother regularly scours the charity shops for old curtains and fabrics to sew up into wild and strange garments. She even started a

fashion label called Wonky Wear and sells her creations on consignment at a number of wacky "alternative" emporiums.

Create kooky gifts for your relatives, or make yourself a belly dancing costume. The world is overflowing with hideous old wedding and bridesmaid dresses. If you use your imagination they can be a rich source of amazing fabrics to chop, splice, hack, recycle and reconstruct into all kinds of fun and outrageous outfits. A one off prom dress for a relative that wants to stand out, a wench's outfit for your next trip to medieval world, or a pirate costume for your spouse. Anything really!

Model Making

If sculpture seems a bit too overwhelming, but you still like the idea of making something three dimensional, model making could be just the thing. Unlike sculptures, which are usually either an artist's abstract creation, or the more conventional 3D likeness of a person, model making is simply the art of creating miniature versions of real things, such as trains, cars or aeroplanes.

While not exactly considered a "high art", model making does require a great deal of skill and patience, particularly if you are designing and creating your own models from scratch. Architects, for example, make the most extraordinary models to bring their visions into 3d form for their clients. However, if you are not into designing you own models, but are more of a specialist in a particular type of car/train/plane or motorbike, there are literally thousands of different model kits available to cater to all tastes and budgets.

Knit With Wit

The artless pastel baby booties and matinee jackets of the past are long gone.

WHAT TO DO IN *RETIREMENT*

Knitting and crocheting have making a bit of comeback in recent times and it no longer means abandoning your wild side. Knitting is now a full on artistic endeavour! All kinds of people are clamouring for beautifully designed original works, and not just in wool. Raffia, slub cotton, spun hemp, mohair, alpaca, jute; all kinds of natural fibres are finding a place in the creative knitter's basket. Knitting needn't be expensive either. You can recycle old jumpers from the thrift store. There are some amazing quality wools lurking in hideous old jumpers that are so out of date that no one in right mind would wear them out in public. You can pick them up for a song and unravel them ready for re-purposing. Why not make something totally outrageous. Here's a challenge, see if you can out-viral the knitting artist Anna Maltz's famous nude suits? (Seriously, you should Google knitted nude suit, and check them out… they are extraordinary!)

Leather-work

Leather-work spans a wide range of aesthetics, from hippy to punk, to high-end designer wear, it offers something for just about everyone, (except of course your die hard vegan). Purses, bags, clothing, wallets, belts, jewellery, shoes, bottle holders, key rings, art works and certain unmentionable "indoor recreational outfits" for British MPs; there are so many things you can make with leather. The tools needed are minimal and relatively inexpensive. All you need is a sharp knife, a hole punch, needles or a sewing machine, sculpting tools and a hammer (for making artistic impressions), buckles and studs as required, and glue.

Make An American Quilt

Whether you get together with friends for a ritual stitch and bitch, or sit quietly quilting, there is no limit to the possibilities for this traditional American art form. There is a vast network of quilters out there, with regular conventions and exhibitions; they even have dedicated websites and chat rooms. Quilters are known for getting together to swap patterns and fabric swatches, and many groups meet up regularly to work on large collective projects.

While making an American quilt is traditionally a quiet and refined activity, it doesn't have to be. There is absolutely no need to stick with the traditional forms. For example Gothic quilting artist Ben Venom is making some truly original pieces that are taking this time-honoured craft into totally

WHAT TO DO IN *RETIREMENT*

uncharted territory. Why not subvert the quilting conventions yourself and make something totally outrageous. Let your imagination run wild. Express your inner world in appliqué!

Jewellery Making

Jewellery can be so much more than just a choking hazard for the grand-kids. It can be a wonderfully unique way to express your self. Whether you go wild with beads, channelling your inner Masai, or drape yourself with gold, silver and diamonds, jewellery is totally fabulous.

It's true, some jewellery making may require extreme heat or hammering, but you can make jewellery out of just about anything. Coloured glass, painted beads, wire, aluminium flashing, epoxy resins, safety pins, buttons, papier-mâché, practically anything can be turned into a body adornment. Pull apart old necklaces and restring them into stunning earrings, beading is dead easy. Make mad pendants. Drape yourself in colour, go nuts! Your young relatives might love to receive a necklace or bracelet that you have made especially for them.

Whittling

Whittling is believed to have been with us since the Middle to Upper Palaeolithic period, when it was the main source of spears and hunting arrows that allowed our ancient ancestors to thrive and survive.

It is also one of the cheapest and most readily accessible crafts around. All you need is a sharp knife and a chunk of wood. "The Art of Manliness" describes whittling as *"a great pastime for the man who wants to craft something, but may not have the room or tools to build a dining room table"*, but this doesn't mean that whittling is just for men. I have a female friend who has created the most extraordinary collection of hand-whittled spoons. She loves the meditative peace and calm of simply working with wood.

Softwoods are the best for beginners because they are considerably easier to cut and shape, whereas hard-woods require a little more patience and skill. Woods with a straight grain tend to give a better result, (as they are considerably easier to work with than woods that have the grain going in multiple directions). Avoid woods with lots of knots, as the knots can cause unwanted irregularities, weaken or even break your work.

WHAT TO DO IN *RETIREMENT*

Lumber yards, craft stores and woodlands where it is permitted to gather fallen branches are all great places to gather supplies. Popular whittling woods are:

BASS WOOD: A soft wood without much grain, basswood has been used by carvers for centuries. In fact German sculptors used to use it for crafting stunning Gothic altarpieces in the middle ages. You can pick up blocks of basswood in most good craft stores, and it's not usually too expensive.

PINE: While a traditional whittling wood, pine has its pluses and minuses. On the plus side it is soft, easy to cut and readily available. On the down side some people feel it doesn't hold detail all that well; and if you are using fresh pine it can be quite sappy, which can leave your fingers and knife quite sticky.

BALSA WOOD: Most of us have some memory of using balsa wood as children. It is one of the mainstays of many crafts, including model making. Balsa is extremely soft, remarkably inexpensive and incredibly flexible. You can use it to make just about anything.

FOUND TWIGS AND BRANCHES: Many people mistakenly believe that you need to buy wood to whittle. This is manifestly not true. Found twigs and branches (from just about any kind of tree) are perfectly suitable for whittling. Sure your creation may be a bit more rustic when you are using random bits of wood but that is all part of the charm.

You don't need a special whittling knife (although they are available). A sharp pocketknife is good enough to get you started.

*WARNING: Even though this goes without saying I am going to say it anyway: When working with sharp knives you need be careful. No one wants to find you covered in blood looking like you just went ten rounds with an axe murderer. Don't rush, take your time, and if you are new to the task take some precautions. A pair of good solid work gloves could go a long way to keeping all your fingers firmly attached to your hands.

Felting

No one is sure whether this ancient eastern craft was first developed in the Middle East or the Far East, but wherever it may have come from no one disputes the fact that FELTING is an age-old practice. Over the centuries

WHAT TO DO IN *RETIREMENT*

felting has evolved into several unique styles, each originating from a different tribe and/or place.

Today felting is practiced by all kinds of people, from nomads on the great plains of Asia (who are still living in traditional felt yurts), to kids in the local kindergarten. There are several simple felting techniques that don't require much in the way of experience or tools, and given the rough and imperfect nature of the form any "mistakes" simply add to the texture and interest of the work.

WET FELTING or FELT MAKING: is the practice of using soap and water on a fibre (most commonly sheep's wool) to make a felted fabric. There is no spinning, knitting, crocheting or weaving involved.

FULLING or KNIT FELTING: is the practice of taking a knitted, crocheted or woven garment and then shrinking it to fill the holes between the stitches. The technique of "fulling" is often used to great effect by those making highly original hats, scarves and wraps.

NEEDLE FELTING: doesn't require soap and water and does not necessarily need to be done with an animal fibre. Needle felting is done by using "felting needles" to apply additional fibres to enhance a fabric or garment (those can be made of felted material or knitted, crocheted or woven material), You can even use it make decorative figurines.

ART FELT is similar to needle felting but, instead of adding fibres to an existing garment you add your fibres onto a special backing paper that dissolves in water. Once you have finished adding your fibres you simply wash your work. The backing paper will dissolve leaving you with just the finished product.

No matter which style or tradition takes your fancy felting is the perfect art form for anyone who likes earthy, natural, random shapes and textures. If you have had enough of straight lines this could well be for you. Felting supplies are readily available on EBay, at your local craft store or in your local shearing shed.

Scrap-booking

Mythologise your family's history by setting out your photos, awards and

WHAT TO DO IN *RETIREMENT*

show tickets in luxurious books filled with pretty coloured cardboard and decorative paper. This is seriously good fun, and takes up much less space in the living room than that overflowing trophy cabinet. You don't have to stop at using photographs and other paper items either. If you want to make your scrapbook a bit more voodoo friendly you could always include things like first-teeth and locks of hair.

Candle Making

Hot wax is good for so much more than just yanking out unwanted body hair. Whether you want to make gifts for the relatives, sell your creations, set the stage for some serious "low-light" romance, or get a lot of burly young firemen to come over, candle making can accommodate. There are so many shapes, colours and scents you can use to create a something that is totally unique to you. Candle making is truly an art form in its own right.

Soap Making

If you are having problems with an under-washed person in your life, handing them a gift of handmade soap, while telling them you would like them to use it and let you know what they think, could be the perfect way to drop them a helpful hint. (It's so much subtler than just shoving a bar of Dove into their hand).

But seriously, soap making is a wonderful way to make original artisan gifts, and it could save you a small fortune come Christmas. This simple, time honoured process can be done with common household ingredients, such as olive oil, coconut oil, Shea butter, goat or sheep's milk, lye, essential oils, flower petals and oatmeal etc. The Internet has countless recipes that you can either follow directly, or use as a base to make your own personal varieties.

*WARNING: Be extremely careful when using lye (AKA: Caustic Soda). It is can cause serious burns in its concentrated form. The first time I made soap I accidentally let a flake of lye fall onto the kitchen bench. When I wiped down the bench to make a sandwich the lye dissolved and ended up being absorbed into the bread. One bite was enough to burn a small welt on my lip. I recommend rubber gloves and putting newspaper down on all surfaces.

Spinning And Weaving

For thousands of years spinning and weaving were the methods we used to make textiles to clothe ourselves. Before spinning and weaving we had to wear animal skins to keep us warm, which was all a bit smelly and draughty. Of course, once we worked out how to make yarns and fabrics our clothing options expanded exponentially. Like so many other artisan crafts, the making of hand-hewn yarns and fabrics is now considered a bespoke art form in its own right. Whether you are spinning up some lumpy alpaca yarn for a scarf or weaving up an intricate tapestry or tartan, spinning and weaving are joyous, meditative, creative pastimes. They are not too taxing on the body. They don't require flaming heat or dangerous chemicals, and the equipment is not prohibitively expensive. You can buy a spinning wheel on EBay for anything from $100 to $1000 dollars and you can pick up a loom from as little as $5 for a kid's craft model. While a serious loom can cost over a

$1000, you should be able to pick up a decent starter loom for less than $150.

Decoupage

For the uninitiated decoupage is the art of decorating three-dimensional objects with images. (At last, a use for all those expired coupons and old copies of National Geographic). Collage is a genuine art form, and can include so much more than just printed images. Found objects, old coins, seed pods, pressed leaves, absolutely anything. There is no limit to the social commentary you can make with some old magazines and a glue stick. You could do an art piece that comments on disposable consumer culture by covering some Ikea furniture with decoupage cuts outs from an Ikea catalogue. (And yes, while that may be a random, pointless suggestion, it would definitely be a talking point).

WHAT TO DO IN *RETIREMENT*

4 HEAD TO YOUR SHED

Man caves, she sheds, everyone loves somewhere they can go and do their own thing. Whether you want to indulge in some creative mechanics, set up a pottery kiln or simply read a book and revel in your solitude, your shed is your haven. It's that magical place where you can do all those messy, filthy, space hungry things that your spouse won't let you do inside the house. A list that includes, but is by no means limited to the following suggestions:

Blacksmithing

Did you know that going back 150 years roughly 20% of census respondents listed their occupation as blacksmith? It's not really that surprising when you think about all the armour, horse shoes, swords, shields, door furniture, hooks, gates, fence posts, plant stands, wheels, barrel strapping, candelabras, hinges, locks and red hot pokers etc., that were forged in personal foundries. However with hand forged items selling at a huge premium these days, people tend to view ironwork as an artisan hobby, (although clearly not one for the feint hearted).

If you are going to take up smiting you are going to need pumping muscles, a strong back, a large well ventilated space, a forge or furnace that can pump out heat of up to 1400 degrees Fahrenheit, (most likely a coal or propane, but propane is much cleaner), some bellows (or a fan for propane), an anvil and hammers, some tongs, some clamps or vices to hold the pieces you are working on, and last but not least some iron to work with. You will also need eye protection, a thick leather apron and gloves, and neighbours who don't mind the sound of you relentlessly pounding on metal.

Glass Blowing

Glass blowing is more than just a way of making homemade trinkets for your

WHAT TO DO IN *RETIREMENT*

cousins bat mitzvah Bomboniere. (Bomboniere are those little gifts given by hosts on special occasions such as bat mitzvahs, weddings, baptisms, first communions or confirmations).

Glass blowing could be your passport to making some truly stunning artistic creations. Unique and colourful beads, bottles, bowls, glasses, goblets, lightshades, marbles, ornaments, paperweights, jewellery, vases and (for those who fancy a bit of hedonism) hookah pipes!

The equipment can be quite expensive, so if there is a studio near you I recommend you try it out before purchasing the necessary accoutrements. If you don't have access to a nearby studio and want to buy a basic kit to try it out you can start with a small torch, like a "Nortel Minor" which should cost less than $200. However, most experienced blowers recommend something with a wider flame, such as a "Major" or a "Red Max" (the wider the flame the greater the range of things you will be able to make), but either of these could set you back $400 or more. You will also need a supply of tank oxygen and propane along with the necessary regulators, and a good supply of glass tubes. You will also need eye protection and good ventilation at the very least. Glass blowing comes with a serious safety warning, molten glass is not something you want to be too casual with.

Lead Lighting

For those that like to see shards of coloured light dancing across their wall, but don't feel inclined to indulge in the necessary mind-altering substances to make it happen, lead lighting could be just the thing. Perfect for solemn religious buildings, period renovations and hippy hang outs, there is nothing sets off a room quite like bits of coloured glass stuck together with lead. Of course making your own is even better. You do not have to rely on one of the many lead light pattern books either. You can design something completely original and off the wall.

There are plenty of instructions and classes out there; you can even learn how to do it on YouTube. You will need some special equipment but nothing that is too expensive. Just some glass, a glasscutter and some lead. Once you get the hang of it, the only tricky part is deciding what patterns and colours to use.

Carpentry

WHAT TO DO IN *RETIREMENT*

Maybe you would like to be more like Jesus, or maybe you are just tired of all those chickens running around loose in the yard? You can kill those two birds with one stone by taking up carpentry and building yourself a chicken coop. From birdhouses to tables and benches, woodworking is an incredibly useful and rewarding skill to have; and if it turns out you are no good at it, remember that just like you Jesus was also a failed carpenter, so you're in mighty fine company!

Motor Mechanics

If you have no mechanical knowledge at all but still find that your car is far too reliable, maybe you could consider doing your own motor vehicle repairs. If you would like to be stranded by the roadside more often I highly recommend getting under the hood with a spanner and just randomly tinkering with things. If that seems like too much of an effort you could always sell your reliable car and buy that old rust bucket that you have always dreamed of. Sure, having an operational car may be practical but where's the fun in that?

Unlikely though it may seem, there are people who would actually like to improve the reliability of their cars. If this is you, you could always enroll yourself in a beginner's class in motor mechanics.

Restoration And Reinvention

You can restore and reinvent just about anything. Turn that dead car into a garden sculpture or a dog kennel! You can cut, hack, stencil, spray, sand, paint, glue and rivet any old junk into useful furniture, sculptural amazements or just plain curiosities. Re-purposing not only stretches the imagination, it makes old things new and exciting again.

Mosaics

Mosaic is one of the few art forms where you get to smash things and make things at the same time. With mosaics you can turn the remains of your last marital plate smashing festival into legitimate art supplies.

Typically made using pieces of broken tiles of various shapes, sizes and colours, mosaics can also be crafted using broken china, glass, coins, metal and plastics among other things. From the traditional Roman style to the weird and wonderful works of Anton Gaudi, (the famous Artist and architect

WHAT TO DO IN *RETIREMENT*

covered the streets of Barcelona in wild ceramic creations), mosaics are a true art form. It's well worth a visit to Barcelona if you need a little extra inspiration.

You can plan out your artwork or just go free form and see what comes out. You can make fantastical garden ornaments that will put your neighbour's gnomes to shame. You could even decorate the side of your house!

Hunters And Collectors

You can collect just about anything. The trick is to take it to the extreme. No matter what it is, if you take it totally over the top a news crew will want to film you and make a story out of it. A word of warning though, collecting can be obsessive so try not to pick something that will aggravate your neighbours or compromise your social cache too much. For example I would avoid collecting such things as dead cars, unspeakably druggy friends, medical waste, toenail clippings, old socks, used band-aids, unwashed underwear and household garbage. Such collections will not only turn you into a social liability but you will also become an environmental hazard. Conversely collecting things like old photographs, Barbie dolls, frog figurines, cookie jars, toy trains and movie posters will be viewed as a cute and curious hobby that may score you a slot in your local paper.

5 THE GREAT OUTDOORS

Tend Your Garden

In the immortal words of Voltaire, "tend your garden". Of course he was speaking figuratively, but it works just as well if you take it literally.

Gardening is incredibly grounding (yes, I know, very droll), and it really doesn't matter if you have a green thumb or not, everyone can grow something. If you are particularly inept when it comes to growing anything green, try planting a weed garden; they practically take care of themselves. You could even offer a lovely bouquet of weeds to your favourite neighbours to say a special thank you when their dog uses your front step as a toilet.

Seriously though, there is mounting research that suggests getting your hands into the dirt, and subsequently coming in contact with the soil bacteria Mycobacterium vaccae, can actually increase your serotonin levels. Serotonin not only strengthens the immune system, it is a noted happy chemical, and a natural anti-depressant, (whereas a lack of serotonin is one of the most noted causes of depression).

A lot of research has been emerging in recent years about how good dirt is for us, and how a dirt-deficiency in childhood could be contribute to conditions such as allergies, asthma and even some mental disorders. So next time you feel like getting down and dirty, don't hesitate. Get out there and get into it.

Grow Your Own Veggies

Fresh food is a total rip off in most supermarkets. First of all it's not usually that fresh, and it tends to be smothered in toxic pesticides. However if you like organic vegetables, saving money and grovelling in the dirt like a hippy, why not plant your own?

It takes less space and effort than you might think, and even if you don't have

WHAT TO DO IN RETIREMENT

a yard you can still grow things in pots on a balcony. Here's an ingenious idea; some women in Africa suspended lengths of large PVC plumbers pipe on a rack. They closed off each end, cut holes in the top and drilled drainage holes in the bottom. They filled them with dirt and planted them out, and they were totally brilliant. They had a rack with about 7 of these pipes stacked up like a book shelf. They where growing all kinds of veggies and herbs, including lettuce, mint and strawberries.

Join A Community Garden

Maybe you fancy something a little more competitive (or social). What about a community garden? What better way to check out whether your squash is bigger than your neighbour's? Many municipalities have community gardens where locals can get an allotment, and if not you could always lobby your local authority to start one.

Community gardens are a stupendous option for anyone who has always wanted a garden but does not have the space. Many community gardens are full of avid swappers, which is just perfect for those who want a marrow and can give a spud. Whether it's swapping cuttings and seeds, chatting about manure (yes you can actually talk crap and have people really appreciate it), or sharing tips on pest control, there is so much to talk about in the garden. The fresh organic veggies are just a small part of being involved; it's the social aspect that is the real gift.

Go Wild With Topiary

For the uninitiated, topiary is the practice of clipping trees or shrubs into ornamental shapes. Contrary to what some people think topiary isn't just for formal gardens in manner houses. You can sculpt all kinds of amazing creatures out of common garden plants, (as was clearly demonstrated in the movie "Edward Scissor Hands"). Some people make such a theatrical feature of their garden that people come from miles around to see and photograph their creations. Whether you like a formal display, geometric shapes, Easter Island style totems, Dr. Seuss like trees or your own zoo full of topiary bears, elephants and giraffes, there is something for every taste. What's more, topiary is not expensive; all you need is a few hedging plants, a good set of pruning sheers and you are up and running. A few good shrubs could keep you going for years.

WHAT TO DO IN *RETIREMENT*

Bonsai Beauty

In the 6th century BC, Japanese students, dignitaries and Buddhist monks would bring back local ideas and practices from their visits to China. Thus the ancient Japanese art of Bonsai developed as an offshoot of the traditional Chinese practice of "penjing", (growing miniature trees in containers). Bonsai is a purely decorative form of cultivation, and its delicate beauty has been said to inspire quiet contemplation and wisdom among spiritual seekers.

Unlike outdoor trees, where the roots can spread out through the soil, the largest bonsai container is usually no bigger than a standard bucket. The largest bonsai will rarely exceed three feet tall, (with the vast majority being significantly smaller). Bonsai's are unquestionably high maintenance, and their successful cultivation can take some time to master. Many of its techniques, such as the selective removal of leaves, the wiring and clamping of branches, and detailed pruning and grafting are quite unique to the form. Working with bonsai's requires specialized tools, a reasonable knowledge of bonsai techniques, and good deal of patience. Regular watering, re-potting and fertilization are absolutely essential.

Cultivating bonsai's is the perfect hobby for anyone who loves plants, but hasn't got access to a garden. To start your own bonsai you will need an open flattish bowl with drainage and specimen of the plant you wish to work with. Many bonsai artists prefer to take a cutting from an old plant, as older plants tend to display a more aged aesthetic. Plants grown from seeds are rarely used.

Plant A Rose Garden

With their decorative and aromatic flowers roses are not just beautiful, they can make excellent burglar proofing when planted under your windows. After all, who in their right mind would brave a rose bush to try and pry open your window?

The successful cultivation of a rose garden takes planning and dedication. Whether you plant standard, long established varieties or try your hand at cross breeding and hybridisation there are a myriad of choices. There are even rose contests for the more competitively minded. And as an added bonus you will never be short of a cheap bouquet on Valentines day.

WHAT TO DO IN *RETIREMENT*

Raise Some Chickens

While you might not win the love of your neighbours with a cow or sheep in your garden, you might be able to keep some chickens. Not only will you enjoy fresh wholesome, cruelty free eggs, but your dogs will just love chasing them around the yard. There are a lot of varieties of chickens to choose from, and they all have different temperaments and abilities; however some of them can be quite homely.

If you are rather shallow or overly image conscious I recommend you ignore the clever ones with good personalities and stick to the air-headed, good-looking chicks. A few drop dead gorgeous "trophy" chickens in your coop will do wonders for your standing at the local agricultural show. While I definitely don't condone such behaviour, if you prefer your chicks "really hot" you could make like Henry the 8th and chop off their heads and cook them. (Although in fairness, I don't think he cooked any of his decapitates).

Whether you want them for dinner or for their eggs, or just for their company chickens are a wonderful addition to any home.

Go Camping, Or Glamping!

Camping is a great way to commune with nature and it can be done at any level. Whether you go wild with a pop up tent and a backpack, or prefer a few more of the rudimentary creature comforts, like beds, cookers and solar powered TV's, camping can accommodate. Why not try the new craze in camping that is taking the world by storm? Glamping, (or "glamorous camping") is a luxury high-end experience especially designed for those that want the escapism, recreation and adventure of camping along with the style and comfort of a five star hotel.

If camping has never really been your thing, but you like the idea of living like a wealthy Bedouin for a few days, glampling might be for you? In some cities they even have rooftop glamping, where you can gaze at the stars while sleeping in a luxury open tent on the top of your local skyscraper.

Although we are only now rediscovering its joys, glamping is not a new concept. There are many noted historical examples. In the sixteenth century, the Duke of Atholl prepared an extreme glamping experience in the Scottish Highlands for King James V's visit. He raised a veritable village of lavish tents

WHAT TO DO IN *RETIREMENT*

and stuffed them with all the luxuries one would expect to find in a royal palace. The Ottomans where also noted glampers. They used to have dedicated teams of artisans travel with their armies just to look after the opulent tents of the imperial generals.

Pack A Picnic

If you are on budget but still want million dollar views with your lunch, there is no better way than packing a picnic lunch. You can picnic just about anywhere. Whether you choose to chow down in a manicured park, at the zoo, on the beach, by the river bank, on the lakeside, by a waterfall or in the city square, picnicking has some big advantages over your local restaurant. For a start, there is no chance there won't be something you like on the menu. You can begin eating whenever you like, as you don't have to wait for the chef to deal with the thirty people that just walked in ahead of you. You don't have to worry about the loud bore at the next table, or withering eye-rolls of arrogant waiters; and you don't have to put up with the selection of Casiotone polkas blasting out from their speakers.

Hobby Farming

If you love the idea of casually working the land and you are not looking to reap vast financial rewards hobby farming could be the perfect solution. Even if you are not keen on selling up and moving to the country, you may still be able to grow some veggies, keep some poultry, rabbits, or even a bee hive if your local authority will permit it. According to Wikipedia, you only need an acre of land to support a couple of milking goats or some pigs. Even if you just love the rural lifestyle but don't want to do much work at all hobby farming, (or homesteading as it is sometimes called), can provide for you. There are plenty of crops, like olives, that require very little in the way of ongoing maintenance; so you can just sit back and let nature do the work.

6 SOCIAL

Pubs And Clubs

While some pubs and bars are clearly depressing pits full of sticky carpet and slot machines, others play host to social groups that regularly meet to eat drink and be merry. There are bars with loyal locals that are a bit like a club, and there are countless actual clubs that have their meetings in local pubs. There are clubs for just about everything imaginable, from chess to cross-dressing. Whatever your proclivity there will be a pub or club out there brimming with like-minded folk that can help you bring your social needs and interests together.

If, for some strange reason, there isn't the club you are looking for in your local area, it is very easy to start one these days. The website "www.meetup.com" operates across the world, with "meetups" for everything from cycling, eating, photography, film buffs, fancy dress, dancing, camping, Kung-Fu, opera, quite literally anything! You can find clubs close to your area, or start a club by signing up and posting a notice. So simple!

Become A Quiz Whiz

What better place to show off that vast accumulation of knowledge than at the local pub quiz? The pub quiz is a long-standing institution, and the perfect environment for smart arses and knows-it-alls. There are not too many places that you can show off how clever you are, eat pub food, and get hammered while you are about it. What could be better?

Chess Clubs

Chess is a wonderful game for those who prefer their warfare cerebral and bloodless rather than violent and visceral, and if you do it in the park you can

WHAT TO DO IN *RETIREMENT*

get your vitamin D hit while you are at it. Chess players tend to be a very earnest and serious lot. Some players are so uptight about winning that they take a small eternity to make a move and get quite sullen and sulky if they lose.

If you are into looking overly intelligent, brooding chin scratching gestures, and generally psyching out your opponents a chess club could be perfect for you. However if you feel like a mindless belly laugh, then maybe not.

Start A Slow Cooking Club

Slow cooking is where it's at these days. Many people are starting their own cooking circles, where once a week a group of people get together to cook something adventurous. Each member of the circle is tasked with bringing certain ingredients and making one part of the meal. While cooking there is much chat and social time, with a large slice of the conversation dedicated to unusual recipes, or what fruits or vegetables should be included in next week's offering. The whole process may take several hours, several bottles of vino, and several hungry mouths to complete.

Vintage Car Clubs

Vintage car enthusiasts are totally nuts when it comes to their cars. Very few parents love their children as much as a car buff will love his mint condition pink and white 1952 Chevy convertible with the tail fins. Car people will abandon all sense of fiscal restraint when it comes to the loving care and maintenance of their prized ride. The level of auto obsession, not to mention spit and polish that goes into getting a vintage car ready for a rally day is simply staggering. If you want to get your partner out of the house and into the garage this is definitely an activity to encourage.

Motorcycle Clubs

Motorcycle clubs come in all shapes and sizes. They are not all the hairy, unwashed outlaws of popular mythology; some are rich and ultra clean. Many Harley riders spend hours polishing their bikes, their leathers, and of course their helmets!

There are clubs out there that are specially for those that no longer have the kids at home, like the Ulysses Club (Australia) a social club for riders over 40, whose membership is dedicated to "growing old disgracefully", or the more

WHAT TO DO IN *RETIREMENT*

family friendly Older Bikers Riding Club that have branches right across the USA.

Then there are your more up market clubs. My husband actually belongs to two clubs; the Ducati club, (a bigger bunch of "mature" successful business people I have yet to meet), and a smaller local club that organises charity events for the local children's hospital.

Film Clubs

If you are a genre nut, or love films of a particular era you could either join or start your own film club. In this day and age, where most people's televisions are bigger than their childhood home, it's not hard to find a venue with a big enough screen to accommodate your weekly offerings. If you want to spread it out beyond your own circle of friends you could always post a notice on local blogs or www.meetup.com and bring a few new bodies into your club; and if you all drink like fish you could probably get the local pub to host it for free!

Join The Medievalists

So lords and ladies, if jousting, lutes, pointy hats and codpieces are your thing the Society for Creative Anachronisms is definitely for you.

If you just love heraldry, chivalry, archery, fancy dress, gnawing meat off the bone, singing madrigals and camping in boggy fields with other medievalists, the SCA has got you covered. These people are FUN, and totally wacky!

Book Clubs

In my limited experience book clubs are excellent places for intellectuals and quasi intellectuals to eat cake and bitch about their partners. With a book club not only are you spared the trauma of deciding which book to read, you can trust the others in the group to reliably tell you what you should to think of the book once you have read it. This can take a lot of pressure off, as you no longer need to form your own opinion. When someone asks what you thought of the book, you can simply parrot the group's assessment. If you do happen to have an opinion that differs from the group it is better to keep it to yourself. Book clubs are a veritable hotbed of "groupthink" and any deviation from the standard line is usually seriously frowned upon.

WHAT TO DO IN *RETIREMENT*

What's Your Game?

Games are totally underrated! You can learn an extraordinary amount playing games, and I'm not just talking about honing your game skills; it's the social, interactive aspects that are totally fascinating. Through games we learn how to be humble in victory and gracious in defeat. We are all told from the time we were old enough to listen, *"it's not whether you win or lose, it's how you play the game"*.

Of course everyone knows winning is the whole point, and that oft repeated platitude is merely there to provide some kind of balm for the losers. But even so, the fear of suffering a humiliating defeat is simply not strong enough to stem our pursuit of irrelevant victories. Whether we admit it or not we all love to play games and we all love to win; even if that means taking our turn as total losers from time to time.

Card Games

Fortunes and friendships have been made and lost over a game of cards. From the meditative isolation of solitaire to the simmering undertones of an intimate bridge party, our card-playing obsession has endured throughout the centuries. From strip poker to black jack, cards have been used as a prelude to romance, a means to fleece the unwary and a simple way to pass the time.

These days there is so much more on offer than just the poker, black jack, bridge, euchre, rummy or cribbage found in "Hoyle's" book of games. There are many new card games available, and some of them are even quite risqué.

Other best selling card games include "Cards against humanity", "Exploding Kittens", "Uno", "Joking Hazard" and my perennial favourite "Munchkin". Munchkin is a strategy card game that has kept my husband and his friends out of my hair for hours at a stretch. Munchkin is so loved and successful by those that play that is now has something like 6,000 expansion packs available. If you're looking for something more intricate and involved than a quick, easy game, Munchkin is the one for you. But be careful though, once you get into it you could become addicted.

Traditional Games

While no one really wants to spend hours doing a Jackson Pollack jigsaw, there are plenty of traditional games that have remained staggeringly popular

WHAT TO DO IN *RETIREMENT*

throughout the ages. Chess, Backgammon, Mah Jong, Chinese Checkers, Drafts, Dominoes, Battle Ships, Hangman, Chess, Yatzee, Jacks, Snakes and Ladders, Ludo and Lego, just to name a few.

Board Games

Unlike computer games board games give you the opportunity to really use your game face. You can psyche out your opponents with your laser like death stare, or try lulling them into a false sense of security with a slightly befuddled look. Board games are like hand to hand combat for the non-combatant.

Some board games are clearly better than others. Mastermind, Dungeons and Dragons, Risk, Cluedo, Pictionary, Trivial Pursuit, Jenga, Connect four, Sorry, Go, Scattergories, Othello, Mousetrap, Kerplunk, Boggle, Twister, Operation, Hungry hippo and Scrabble, are all amazingly great!

Monopoly on the other hand has always been a bit of a worry. My entire childhood memory of Monopoly was that it generally began well, but pretty soon descended into one player exhibiting all the voracious greed of a Russian oligarch. Everyone else would become increasingly despondent, until finally someone petulantly tossed their piece across the room and declared they weren't playing anymore. (Not really my idea of fun).

WHAT TO DO IN *RETIREMENT*

7 GOING SOLO

Solo Games

Rubik's Cubes, Crosswords, Sudoku, Solitaire, Free-cell, Word Finder puzzles and Totem Tennis are all great ways to fill in a few odd minuets, or even sharpen up your grey matter when travelling solo. My favourite game for exercising the mind when I am on my own is "Boggle". Boggle is not strictly speaking a solo game, but I like to challenge myself. It is played by shaking a covered tray of 16 cubic dice, each with a different letter printed on each of its sides. The dice fall into a tray where only the top letter of each cube is visible. You have three-minutes in which to search for words that can be constructed from the letters of sequentially adjacent cubes, ("adjacent" cubes are those horizontally, vertically, and diagonally neighbouring). Of course, being a word person I love Boggle almost as much as Scrabble!

Computer Games

Computer games can be as simple as solitaire, or they can be highly complex virtual worlds in which you can interact with millions of other players in real time, all from the privacy of your own room. Whether you are playing a game for one, challenging a computer generated opponent or entering a virtual world, like 'World of Warcraft' to 'Second Life' millions of people log on every day to play their favourite games. Beware though, it can be highly addictive!

Dance The Night Away

Tango anyone? Did you know that in Buenos Aires you can see 70 year-olds tangoing in the street at two in the morning? From the spiced up Latin rhythms of the cha cha, to the refined formality of a waltz dancing is a great way to get yourself into the arms of a stranger (or your partner if you prefer).

WHAT TO DO IN *RETIREMENT*

Whether you love a sizzling samba, a jumping jive, a punk pogo or a mindless macarena, there is a dance for practically every taste and musical preference, Hit the mosh pit, form a tap dancing troop, or go strictly ballroom. If you are feeling particularly sexy and adventurous you could even try the waist-trimming roll of a belly dance class to get you moving. Even if you can't dance you can still hit the floor; just make up your own moves. Who knows, you might even enjoy hurling yourself about with a random flailing of limbs. Whichever way you do it, dancing is a great way to get fit and have fun; and if you really are truly awful at it just think of the joyous laughter your moves can give to others. So why not get off the couch and get your endorphins pumping? What could be more social than dancing?

8 MUSICAL

Not only is music is one of the most enjoyable aspects of life, there is mounting evidence that playing music helps to keep the mind sharp. Most sensory inputs only activate one localized area in the brain, but music sparks neural activity all over the place, simultaneously firing up the areas of the brain that process sound, memory, attention, language, sight, touch and more. Music brings these separate centres together in a way few other experiences can.

Learn A Musical Instrument

For those who would like to try their hand at playing an instrument you will be pleased to know it is not as difficult as you might think. You can go the self-taught route, take some lessons, or even sign up for an online course. The wonderful thing about playing a musical instrument is that it makes you feel totally euphoric; and once you have your instrument it costs you absolutely nothing. These days, with advanced robotic manufacturing, you can find a wide variety of cheap, quality instruments, either on EBay or on the High St. There has never been a better time to get yourself that musical instrument you have always dreamed of.

If you love music you can quite literally play for several hours every day. Not only does playing music provide countless hours of totally absorbing activity, it boosts your levels of dopamine, (a chemical that regulates the pleasure and rewards centres within the brain). It's a far better high than throwing back a few beers.

Oh, and as an added bonus a lot of musical instruments give you a fair workout into the bargain; and not just the drums, playing guitar or piano can burn a lot of calories too.

WHAT TO DO IN *RETIREMENT*

Sing A Song

Whether you want to join a band, a choir, or go chanting in a Hindu temple, singing is an incredible feel good experience, and it's amazingly good for your health too. It will keep your endorphins pumping while keeping your lungs fit and active. Even if you are not up for singing in a public you can still have an amazingly good time warbling in the shower.

If you fancy your self as a bit of a crooner you could download some karaoke midi files and invite your friends over for a sing along. You can find a midi file for practically any song you can think of somewhere on the net, so you should have no trouble finding your favourites. Most times you can find the lyrics on Google as well.

"http://www.midaoke.com/" has an enormous catalogue of songs for free.

* A midi file is a backing track that will usually play back on your computer. Although you may need to Google and download a midi file player.

However, if you need a bit more confidence to get you out of your shell you might consider taking a lesson or two. Whether you want to sing opera, heavy metal or yodelling you way through the day, there is no need to keep that voice hidden in the bathroom. You can either find a teacher, (although lessons can stretch the budget), or sign up for an online course, where one payment buys you a course of lessons for life.

I recommend you check out the Singing Zone:

"https://www.thesingingzone.com/sing-with-freedom" (I don't have any association with this vendor, and get no kick back from sales).

Alternately, if you have a sense of humour about it, you could always turn your self into a comedic parody of a singer. That way you can have a successful singing career, (even if you are way over 40), and you don't have to be any good at all. Just Google up "Wing singer", or "Margarita Pracatan" and check these ladies out. If they can do it, so can you! (Seriously, check them out; they are jaw dropping!)

Join A Choir

Choirs are a wonderfully social option, and a great way to ease into the sing of things; after all there is safety in numbers. If you like the gospel gowns and love listening to everyone else singing around you, but are worried that people might start writhing in pain as soon as you open your mouth, you could always do what my mother does and just mouth the words. It's not really cheating if you are having fun.

Open Mic Nights

Music is highly social. Even if you are not ready to join a band there is usually an open mic night or a jam session or two in every town. And even if you don't feel up to getting up on stage yourself it's an excellent place to get involved with the local scene and meet people that you can maybe jam with at home.

Write A Song

I love song writing. I have been doing it since I was about 8 years old and have written hundreds of songs over my lifetime. I even taught a class in it once. You don't need to be proficient at playing an instrument; in fact you really don't need to know anything much about music at all. You don't even need three chords, as there are plenty of fabulous two chord songs about!

The main thing with song writing is to let it flow. It's about getting the lyrics together in a way that matches the tone and tempo of the music. There are many software programs – like the Real Book app, Band in a Box, or Garage Band- that can take care of the music side for you, leaving you free to pen anything from a love song to punk anthem.

It really is dead easy. Just bang together a quick computer backing track, or make a slight adjustment to the chords of a song you like and you are free to warble and express your self until something good falls out. I recommend trying to write the WORST song you possibly can to get you started. It's a great fun exercise, and you can compare your best worst efforts with a friend.

Once you have done something truly awful and shared it over a laugh, you are then free to express yourself without inhibition; letting those 95 truly rancid ideas flow through to get to the 5 good ones! As soon as you are comfortable with the idea that not every word you write has to be brilliant, you can have an absolute ball with song writing. If you let 100 ideas flow out, chances are at least one or two of them will be good. Like this, line after line, build up your

WHAT TO DO IN *RETIREMENT*

words and melody until voilà! A song!

Once you have a few songs written you could book a studio and record them, or just lay them down on your computer. You could even upload them to iTunes for sale, or convert one into your ring tone.

9 LITERARY

Dive Into Literature

The pen is mightier than the sword. Which is rather convenient when you take into account the high price and relative inaccessibility of swords; and the fact that you can buy a pen at the local shop for under a dollar.

Of course, these days writing with a keyboard is considerably quicker and easier. But no matter what means you use to get your words out, you can weave together whole worlds from pure imagination. Your words can be challenging, inspiring, confronting, or whimsical, anything really. Whether it's the story of Fred the flying amoeba or your personal political manifesto, there is no reason to keep your thoughts hidden from the page indefinitely. Get writing!

Write A Novel Or A Screen Play

Statistically speaking 100% of people have a great idea for a novel or screenplay. (If you don't believe me take a straw poll at the next party you attend). This means that simply by virtue of being human you must have at least one story you are burning to tell. Why not take the opportunity to get yours out onto the page? You don't have to produce a word-perfect first draft. You simply have to let the ideas flow. The spit and polish can come later, when you get into editing. There are some wonderful books to help you learn how to construct a story and get you started. I recommend Joseph Campbell's "The Hero's Journey" or Robert McKee's "Story".

Write A Short Story

If you are too lazy or just too impatient to write a whole novel why not go for the speedy alternative and pen a short story. Did you know that the master of

WHAT TO DO IN *RETIREMENT*

creepy and weird, Edgar Allen Poe mostly wrote short stories? In fact he only ever wrote one novel. But seriously, short stories are a wonderfully liberating form. You can explore the intricate nuances of a single idea in one succinct piece, or put together a collection to explore a theme from several different angles.

Start A Blog Or A Vlog

Blogging is a fantastic way to have to your say. Doesn't matter what the topic, if you blog it, someone will read it! A blog is an online journal/publication that is usually (but not always) dedicated to a particular topic. There are many websites that will host your blog for FREE. One of the best and most popular is Wordpress. There are lots of online tutorials on Youtube so if you are not sure how to do it just Google up the information you need. Just visit "www.wordpress.com" and sign up for a free account

If you are craving more fame, and would like to turn yourself into a celebrity cult figure you could go wild on your very own video blog (called a "vlog"). The idea is the same as a blog but instead of writing you talk into a video or camera and upload it to Youtube. People love wild and weird Vlogs. You can go so much further than with just the written word, you can wear strange outfits, build yourself a set and let your personality shine through in the most direct way possible.

WHAT TO DO IN *RETIREMENT*

Send Letters To The Editor

If you have plenty of opinions to share around this is a really fun activity. You can take issue with a particular columnist, (some of them make it so easy), or you can just criticize and condemn with utter impunity.

If you find your letters are not making it into the mainstream papers as often as you would like, you could always try your hand at blog comments. Comments are a great medium for passionately opinionated people who don't feel up to writing and maintaining their own blogs; they are also a fabulous outlet for habitual trolls.

Write Your Biography

Turn all those priceless anecdotes your family no longer want to hear into literary gold. If you are living a fascinating life why not share the unique intricacies of your personal story with the world? If you don't want to take the time off from your adventures you could always dictate it and have it transcribed, or you could even hire a ghost-writer. Upwork is full of them. www.upwork.com

Get Down With A Poetry Slam

From the Shakespearean highbrow of *"Shall I compare thee to a summer day?"*; to the immortal bathroom classic *"Here I sit broken hearted "*

Poetry is everywhere.

From the humble limerick to a wistful haiku, from gangster rap to a lover's sonnet there are so many forms and meters to poetry. You could write just about anything and declare it poetry; there simply are no rules. (Well, except for the forms that have rules that is, which of course is most forms, but you don't have to obey them!)

When I was a teenager I joined a colourful band of "street poets", aged 14-80. We used to print out our poetry and hand it out for free to passers by on the street. We handed out hundreds of poems everyday and it never failed to raise a smile.

Of course, there is no law that says you have to hand out the fruits of your literary labour for free. I once purchased a spontaneously written poem from a guy with an old typewriter who was "poetry busking" on Fisherman's Wharf (in San Francisco). My immediate thought was that every city and town NEEDS someone doing this. Maybe that someone could be you?

Read Through Your Bookshelf

Everyone has that list of books they always wanted to read but never had the time. Well, now you do! Why not take some time to relax and work your way through that library that has been gathering dust on the bookcase.

Join The Local Library

This is kind of a no brainer. Libraries will lend you books to read for free, which is amazing. There is no excuse for not joining and making use of the incredible resource. Even if you're not that into books, many libraries have all the latest magazines on racks so you can read them for free. They also tend to have some of the best notice boards around. Anything going on in the neighbourhood, from free concerts to free medical screenings will usually find it's way onto the library notice board.

WHAT TO DO IN *RETIREMENT*

10 EDUCATIONAL

Give Yourself A First, Second Or Third Degree

OK, your friends may think you are already a bit of a know-it-all, but why not add some letters to your title. BA, MBA, MA, Phd? It's all good stuff at a dinner party! If you enrol yourself in an undergrad class you may even get to hang out with some lovely folk who are still young enough to know everything. Lucky you!

It doesn't have to be seriously expensive Ivy League study either. There are plenty of online universities, scholarships and community colleges out there offering affordable or even free studies. In fact Germany just made its University tuition free for everyone, no matter what country you come from.

Also many colleges and universities now offer courses on line. Why not check out "Stanford Online" (online.stanford.edu/), or EdX (https://www.edx.org/) which provides information and links to some of the best free university courses from places like MIT, Berkeley UC, Caltech, Dartmouth, Princeton, Cornell, Boston University, Imperial College London, Australian National University, The University of Tokyo plus a whole lot more. Many of them even offer free courses. For example it's well worth checking out what is available from the Harvard open learning Initiative, (www.extension.harvard.edu/open-learning-initiative).

Self Educate

Many of the smartest and most successful people in the world didn't finish high school. Which really isn't all that surprising, as formal education is not always a great option for a curious mind. If you are an unconventional thinker, have interests that lie outside the mainstream, or simply can't afford formal study, you can always do it yourself.

WHAT TO DO IN *RETIREMENT*

Maybe you are curious as to how the assassination of one Arch Duke led to the deaths of over 37 million people? Perhaps you have wondered what Einstein was talking about when he coined the term "Spooky action at a distance"? Maybe you feel a pressing need to brush up on your knowledge of the mating habits of the sea cucumber? Even for those who don't have the Internet at home, there are still public libraries, and many of them have computers and free Internet access, so you can quench that nagging thirst for knowledge.

Join A Debating Club

Not only is debating great for anyone who loves a good argument, it is seriously educational. When you are given a position to argue you will need to do significant research to mount a compelling case. But it's not just your research that can teach you a thing or two, you get to hear all the information and interpretations brought to subject by the other debaters. It's is a great way to stretch your thinking out beyond your own assumed positions and opinions.

Sit In On A Free Lecture

Many universities and colleges have a regular program of free public lectures. They usually try to present on a wide range of topics, so you shouldn't find it too hard to find one that appeals. Just recently my husband and I attended a fascinating series of six lectures on astrophysics. They even provided tea and biscuits (cookies???). We learned some interesting dinner party facts and got to meet some interesting people during the break. Check out the tertiary institutions in your area, I am sure they will have something on offer that is too good to miss.

Know Nothing And Do It Anyway

AKA the school of fake it till you make it. Just do it. What ever it is have a go, you will very soon learn what works and what doesn't. Often those that forego any knowledge or formal training will come up with new techniques and innovative ways to do things that they never would have thought of if they had been trained. Abandoning accepted protocol is so much fun. Why not throw away the recipe and just guess, why not colour outside the lines? Admittedly the results may be a disaster but equally you might find yourself becoming the originator of a new form. Nothing ever got invented by following the pattern.

WHAT TO DO IN *RETIREMENT*

Get on line and check out "the bush mechanics", a group of inspired folk from the Australian outback who live in such a remote location that they have learnt how to use things like tree branches to fix the broken axle in their car.

11 POLITICAL

There is nothing quite like the cut and thrust of a good debate. Whether it's hurling insults across the chamber, or banging fists at the dinner table, politics is a passionate pursuit. If you want to tax the billionaires, champion the middle class, kick the poor or save the planet then politics is definitely for you.

Join A Political Party

If you genuinely want to do more to further your own ideals, how about joining a political party? Don't be fooled by the term "party". I can assure there is nothing light or frivolous about these parties. Yes, it's true their primary obsession may be handing out leaflets, but they are also pretty good for sharpening up the old Machiavellian manoeuvres.

Why not start your own party? A political party is a fabulous choice for anyone who loves power, intrigue and indulging themselves in incessant arguments.

Go Green!

If you just love being self-righteous, shaming your friends, or calling out total strangers on their wasteful and selfish ways, then going green is going to be heaps of fun for you.

Not only will going green save you money, help reduce pollution and preserve the living environment, you will get to glare scornfully at those ignorant folk who failed to bring their own bags to the supermarket. You can even switch other people's lights off in the middle of the day and give them earnest sermons about how wasteful they are. The best part is that you will be right, and they will know it.

WHAT TO DO IN *RETIREMENT*

Lobby For Your Cause

Does the idea of making a difference in the world appeal to you? Maybe you think that the world has far too many of those pesky wind farms and you want to do something about it. Maybe you want to stop those poor coal miners becoming endangered? Well why not start a lobby group to advocate for them?

There are so many great causes to choose from. Lowering taxes for billionaires and multinational corporations, (although to be fair they have well established gaggle of lobbyists already working on their cause); striking Darwin's theory of evolution from the high school curriculum; you can lobby for practically anything,

Lobbyists have helped to change many laws all over the country. You don't need to have any special skills, knowledge or intelligence to lobby, but you do need to be passionate about your cause. What's more, when you surround yourself with other lobbyists who share the exact same ideas and opinions as you, you can avoid ever being challenged on your beliefs. Happy days!

12 VOYEURISTIC

I Like To Watch

Watching, viewing, looking, leering, peering, peeking, gawking, gazing, glimpsing, glancing, staring, perving or just keeping an eye on things. The pleasures of the human eye are immeasurable. Whether one is staring into a flickering fire, cheering on the game, sauntering through the Guggenheim, taking in a show or trolling the Internet for questionable content, simply watching things is one of our greatest human joys.

Go Train Spotting

Train spotting is bags of fun for obsessives. Spotters spend countless hours trying to land an eyeball on all kinds of different types of rolling stock. It is not uncommon for train spotters to form small prides and exchange notes on their spots, and where and when they saw them.

Many spotters like to photograph the carriage and serial numbers or record them in log books. Unfortunately, due to the fact that every second person is planning to blow up some public utility or the other these days, photographing trains has become somewhat frowned on, (and doubly so if you happen to be wearing a burqa at the time); but you shouldn't let the spectre of being indefinitely detained as a terrorist suspect deter you. Train spotting really is fabulous. If you would like a lower risk alternative, try visiting a train museum. You can spot all kinds of old world rolling stock without fear of becoming a terror suspect.

Enjoy A Spot Of Bird Watching

Bird watching first appeared as a gentleman's pastime in Victorian times, where observing birds for purely aesthetic reasons was considered a luxury of the well fed. Everyone else viewed them as a potential meal.

Bird watching is an excellent pastime for those with voyeuristic tendencies, as you can quite legitimately get about with binoculars slung around you neck without raising any suspicions. Thankfully not all bird watchers have a proclivity for taxidermy, which is the somewhat gruesome habit of stuffing and mounting dead animals.

Become A Star Gazer

If you love telescopes, observatories and cloudless desert nights, stargazing could be for you. Maybe you're worried that you might be a bit narcissistic and self- important? Well nothing can make you feel quite as insignificant as the sheer vastness of the cosmos. But apart from its obviously humbling aspects, astronomy is also a great hobby for vampires, (or anyone else that finds they are unable to face the daylight hours).

However, if you would rather inflate, rather than deflate your ego, astronomy can help with that too! How about having a star named after you? (Or your significant other). Admittedly paying to have this done is largely a scam by unscrupulous Internet entrepreneurs, but you don't have to line their pockets.

WHAT TO DO IN *RETIREMENT*

You can just pick a star, make up a name, print up a certificate and hang it on your wall, (or tie it up with a pretty ribbon and give it to your partner).

Check Out Museums And Galleries

Museums and galleries are well worth travelling for. You should see the works of Van Gough, Leonardo DaVinci and the fossilized remains of a trilobite at least once in your life. It is simply staggering what they have in museums, it's like walking into another world. Mini snuff boxes from the court of Queen Elizabeth the first, the Apollo moon capsule, the Elgin Marbles, Rodin's Thinker, three thousand year old Greek pottery, the Ishtar gates, really silly animatronic dinosaurs; all of these things I have seen in museums.

A tree made of guns, a Gaultier bustier, the terracotta army, Jackson Pollack's Blue poles, Andy Warhol soup cans, and some esoteric installation piece by Claudia Luenig (my incredible artist friend from Vienna), all of this has been served up to my eyeballs in Galleries. Mind boggling ideas, staggering inspirations, incredible artistic skill, it's all out there on show in your local gallery.

Do The Zoo

While I love looking at the lions, seeing the seals, gazing at gazelles, taking in the tigers and meandering past the meerkats, going to the zoo is always a tainted pleasure for me. Fortunately many modern zoos have gone to great pains to make wonderful enclosures and naturalistic environments for the animals, but it is tragic that animals that should be free are locked in cages.

The sad truth is that we have made a bit of a mess of things and many of these animals now need our help to survive. As we've messed up their world I think the least we can do is lend our support to their survival; and one of the best ways we can do this is to visit our local zoos. The ticket price will help fund efforts to stave off extinction and disease, so it's well worth it. There is a great deal to be learned from our animal friends, and what better way to learn it than to pay them a visit?

Take In A Show, Or Two!

From top end productions to local theatre groups, arts festivals and street performers, most cities and towns have a wealth of entertainment on offer. Sure you can lash out on a Broadway show, but that's far from all that's out

WHAT TO DO IN *RETIREMENT*

there. Try exploring the off-beat world of fringe theatre and off Broadway style selections in your local area.

Whether it's a burlesque cabaret, a stand up comedy night, a theatre sports round or an amateur Tennessee Williams play, live shows are exciting. If you want to make sure that you don't miss out, why not sign up for an entertainment company's mailing list, so they can let you know when something fun is on. www.citysearch.com usually has local listings for all kinds of things.

Film Festivals

If you love long agonizing films about awful people, films that don't have any discernible plot line, or even films that you just don't understand, then your local film festival might be just the thing.

I know it is difficult to find these types of films at the local cinema, but don't worry film festivals are full of them! While there are some festivals that specialize in specifically "entertaining" genres, (like comedy or science fiction), the vast majority are totally dedicated to wrist-slashingly turgid dramas that are almost too painful to watch. Festival films have even been known to induce audience members to spontaneously suicide, so this is no place to go if you are emotionally fragile.

But seriously while about 80-90% of festival films may be a tad on the torturous side, it's the 10-20%, those gems that you won't see anywhere else that make it well worth taking a punt on the price of ticket. There is also that special sense of community you feel when you sit in the dark with other people totally absorbed in a story. It's like being gathered around an ancient camp fire staring into the flickering light while someone weaves a magical tale.

Enjoy Some Live Music

WHAT TO DO IN *RETIREMENT*

13 PERFORMING

Show Me

Performing artists have been pushing the boundaries of human understanding throughout recorded history. Whether you resonate with the tragic humanity of Shakespeare and Chekov, the startling visuals of Cirque d' solei, or the pulsing lights and wild beats of your local DJ, there are so many things out there to see and hear. Participating in a live show can open up your mind to new possibilities. It can smash your fears and change the way you see, hear and process information. Once you lose your fear, you will find every live performance you experience has the capacity to alter your perceptions; both of yourself and the world around you. Getting involved in the performing arts is one of the best ways to stretch the bounds of your imagination.

Lights, Camera, Action

Your relationship with film doesn't have to be limited to just being a consumer. If you have a megaphone, a riding crop, a director's chair, a video camera or a smart phone, then you are well on the way to becoming a film-maker. You won't even need actors if you have a cat, (although just like a temperamental actor your cat will probably refuse to take direction, demand better food and agitate for a bigger trailer).

Si Fi, horror, romance, comedy, a heart warming family birthday? Whatever the genre you can have a go. Write a script. Turn your spare room, the local park, or the local pub into your movie set. Ask around, I am sure you will find no shortage of amateur actors who would love to star in your film. Maybe documentary or cinema veritie is your thing? In which case just grab your camera, go people watching and film life as it happens.

Most computers come with some form of free movie editing software such as

WHAT TO DO IN *RETIREMENT*

i-movie, and if not there is plenty of free movie editing software that can be downloaded from the Internet. There's plenty of royalty free music you can use in programs like Garage Band, so you can get a cool soundtrack going without worrying about whether you just became a pirate.

There are so many ways to get your videos and films seen. Not only are there regular short film nights in most cities and large towns, there are hundreds of short film festivals throughout the world that you can enter your film into.

Move Over Ted Turner

If you decide to create your own films or videos, what better way to share them with the world than putting them up online? Why not start your own YouTube channel? (In case there is anyone out there who doesn't know this already, YouTube is a video-sharing site where people from all over the world post their own video and films for people to see). It is very easy to make your own YouTube channel and it costs you nothing. You could even make your own television-style talk show, news and op-ed show or even a craft, hobby or cooking show.

Once you have established your channel you can ask well-known locals or semi-famous people to guest on your show. You never know, your channel might become a huge hit around the world! You tube now has paid advertising so if you make a popular show you could also end up supplementing your income.

Make Some Magic

Magicians have been delighting audiences for centuries. Of course, these days they are mostly found at kid's birthday parties, but that is no reason not to learn a few tricks. If you get your performance skills up you could even put on the odd show. Admittedly, a lot of magic tricks require specialist equipment; but if you have a top hat and are in possession of a lazy rabbit who is just lying around mooching off you, then why not put them to work? Personally I have yet to master much in the way of magic, but I have learned how to make my money disappear without a trace!

Amateur Theatre

Acting is a perfect pastime for the relentlessly self-obsessed. If you love showing off, kissing co-stars that you don't really like and generally being a

WHAT TO DO IN *RETIREMENT*

total drama queen this one is definitely for you. Perfect for the frustrated Thespian or would be theatrical costumer. Local amateur theatre is a wonderful place to live out that dream of being on the stage. Even if (like me) all you get to do is play a dancing cardboard box under a giant Christmas tree, you can still tread the boards.

Amateur theatre also offers plenty of opportunities for people who prefer being behind the scenes. Directors, producers, graphic artists, lighting designers and operators, set designers and builders, stand by props people, costumers, sound mixers, stage managers, people to sell tickets and usher in the audience; even fawning fans to pump the star's ego, all of these people are required to pull off a successful production.

Puppetry

Puppetry is the perfect pastime for control freaks and manipulators. Not only do you get to play master of the (puppet) universe, people may well applaud you for your efforts.

Puppetry has been adored by audiences of all ages since as far back as the sixteenth century. The English fairground classic "Punch and Judy", and the traditional Japanese puppet theatre "Bunraku" stand as living testaments to puppetry's timeless appeal. However, in more recent times some rather adventurous Australian gentlemen have turned their private parts into "puppets", regularly touring the globe with their aptly named show "Puppetry of the Penis"! I kid you not… if you don't believe me, Google it! What's more, they have even trained up a squad of game young gentlemen to perform their lewd form of puppetry at hen's parties. Personally, I don't recommend you try this, it seems like it might be painful and I'm not sure it would go down too well with the relatives.

Leaving aside Australia's somewhat controversial contribution to the art form, putting on a puppet show is a thoroughly engaging creative pursuit that requires all the skills of a full on theatre production. You could try your hand at scriptwriting, directing, or set and costume design. Throw in a bit of ham acting and a few bad jokes and you are up and running. What's more, you can put on a puppet show in a space no bigger than a cardboard box. Why not put on a performance for you local primary school, the local nursing home or even at the grand-kid's birthday party?

WHAT TO DO IN *RETIREMENT*

There are several types of puppets you can easily make at home, such as finger puppets, glove puppets (like lamb chop), marionettes (like the Thunderbirds), stick puppets (like Kermit), or if you are a bit more ambitious you could even try constructing a full body puppet like the ones used in the Lion King. Of course, you don't have to make or be your own puppet. EBay is teeming with all kinds puppets in all price ranges and budgets.

Stand Up Comedy

Good comedy never gets old. Think of all the amazing comics aged over 50, that slay them in isles. Think John Cleese, Jerry Seinfeld, Wanda Sykes, Whoopi Goldberg, John Stewart, Stephen Colbert, Joe Brand, Alan Davis, Stephen Fry, Phil Jupitus and Sandi Toksvig. Remember the great George Carlin, Phyllis Diler, Lucille Ball and Joan Rivers. Not to mention all the incredible 40 something comics like Tina Fey, Amy Pohler, Margret Cho, Samantha Bee and Chelsea Handler that are showing no signs of slowing down any time soon.

You don't have to have had a long career to try your hand at comedy. If you can make people laugh you will be welcomed just about anywhere. Take the inspiring example of Chuck Esterly. At 89 years of age Chuck decided that he had put his comedy dream on hold long enough, so he took to the stage and performed his very first stand up gig, and he totally crushed it! As soon as his routine hit YouTube it went viral, raking up over half a million views! If you need a bit of extra inspiration to get you motivated, you really should check him out. (Just Google "Chuck Esterly", and you will find him).

Ventriloquism

If your sense of humour is a tad on the harsh side, then what better way to express your antisocial fantasies than delivering a spray of insults under the guise of ventriloquism? If you have a long harboured desire to taunt your friends and family, and have them applaud you for it, ventriloquism is the answer.

Ventriloquism is not just for performers. If you have an unpleasant truth you want to get off your chest, but you lack the courage to come out and say it, why not get your very own "Chucky" doll do the talking for you! No matter how grievous it is, you can get away with saying just about anything with a dummy on your knee!

WHAT TO DO IN *RETIREMENT*

Clowning Around

Clowning is not just for paedophiles, psychopaths, serial killers, street performers and children's entertainers. Clowning is enduring staple of the circus arts that has been delighting audiences for centuries. After all, where would Cirque du Soleil be without the fire juggling, plate spinning, ball walking, horn blowing, face painting antics of their clowns?

Whether you pay homage to the classic black and white style of Pierrot, the green hair of Herschel Krusty, the dazzling diamonds of Harlequin, the jaundiced robes of Ronald McDonald, the flaming red nose and electrified hair of Bozo, or invent your own original freak faced prankster, donning a clown's persona is a totally liberating process. The moment you get the grease paint on you are not longer playing by the same rules. Once you have your clown face sorted, all you have to do is add a few circus skills to your repertoire and you could be juggling at the local fair or making balloon animals for feral children parties.

Turn Yourself Into Performance Art

Performance art is all about getting out there and doing it. Put a flash mob together and tango through your local shopping mall. You could get an outrageous outfit and turn yourself into a living statue, like one of the living sculptures on the Rambles promenade in the centre of Barcelona.

If your costume is amazing enough you can simply take a seat in a tourist precinct and people will quite literally give you their money. Performance art doesn't have to be formal or structured; it could be anything at all.

The thing about performance art is it requires you to detach yourself from your ego, and any ideas about how you are perceived in the world.

WHAT TO DO IN *RETIREMENT*

14 HEDONISTIC

Eat it... Just eat it

Cook with weird implements. Buy a wok or a Moroccan tajine, break out the fondue set or cook your fish in a banana leaf! Fry an egg on your engine! The ways to prepare food are limitless, so why stick with the ones you know.

Eat International

Goat curry? Deep-fried crickets? Bull's penis? (Yes I said it). OK, so maybe you don't want the bull's penis, but seriously, there is a world of extraordinary foods out there just waiting for you! Whether it's main courses you have never tried, or desserts you never knew existed the world is a veritable smorgasbord of weird and wonderful tastes and textures. Mix it up, try something you love but done a little bit differently. Instead of potato chips, try sweet potato or taro chips. Go wild with weird chocolate, whether it's chilli chocolate, chocolate coated coffee beans or chocolate covered ants, (yes they do make them). Why not give your regular restaurant a miss and try eating something that you might think is odd. Other than the possibility of food poisoning and death, (which is a risk you actually face whenever you eat anything), what's the worst thing that could happen?

I highly recommend you add these international culinary amazements to your bucket list.

Malaysian: Curry laksa, Nasi goereng, Mee Goereng. **Thai:** Pad Thai, Laab, Green curry coconut. **Indian:** Malai kofta, Dahl makani, Palak paneer, Aloo Gobi. **Japanese:** Tempura, Udon, Sushi **French:** Olive Roulade, Escargot, Oursins. **Italian:** Arancini, Angalotti. **Swiss:** Rösti (Swiss fried potato, that could be the original hash brown).

WHAT TO DO IN *RETIREMENT*

Greek: Dolmades, Taramosalata. **Middle Eastern:** Falafel balls, Homos Dip, Baba ganoush. **UK:** Baked beans on toast, Mashed potato, Yorkshire or Black Pudding. **Australian:** Pumkin soup, Vegamite toast (spread thin).

Sweets

Italian: Tiramisu, Florentines, Panforte, Cannoli (Ok I know you have tried them already but they really are totally amazing and you should have them again). **French:** Crème brûlée, augnarde, croquembouche, Cachou lajaunie, Fraise tagada, Eclaire. **Indian:** Laddu, Jalebi, Gulab Jamin, Ladoo. **Greek:** Halva, Greek Vanilla. **Mexican:** Chocolate covered coffee beans.

Thai: Khanom Gluay (Banana Treat) Durian Coconut Milk Soup with Sticky Rice, Banana Leaf Sticky Rice, Fried Banana with Roasted Rice.

If you can't find anything weird and wonderful to excite your tongue locally why not head for somewhere more exotic? Travel to your nearest big city where there are foods from all nations. You could even travel the world on a global gobble fest.

The Cafe Crawl

The cafe crawl is an essential part of life for any cosmopolitan urban sophisticate. Drag your friends to sample and discuss the finer points of Arabica coffee beans, Kona verses Kenya, cappuccino verses a flat white, espresso verses macchiato; critique the decor, the relative skills (and hipster man bun) of the barrista, and generally enjoy the cafe experience. Take your laptop and write that novel while you are there.

The cafe is the perfect environment for socialising with friends, people watching, chatting up strangers, reading a good book, ranting about politics and philosophy, or just generally looking cool and hanging out. However, if you live in a cafe poor area you could always travel to one of the world's great "cafe" cities, Paris, Rome, Vienna, Milan or somewhat surprisingly Melbourne Australia, which has more cafes per head of population than any other city in the world, and has been voted as having the "world's best coffee".

If tea is more your thing you may find a lot of cafes prove disappointing; however a quick trip to the UK and you can travel the country top to bottom while never being more than spitting distance from a phenomenally good tearoom. English tearooms are famous for their scones (no, they not the same as the American ones) with jam (Jelly) and cream, gingham tablecloths and laid back (slow) service.

Drink And Be Merry

It is an indisputable fact that most people love to drink. In some places it borders on a national obsession. The love of alcohol has been with humanity since the very beginning; even our apish cousins are happy to imbibe by gorging themselves on fermenting fruit.

Now, I am not advocating for working oneself into an alcoholic stupor, or hanging out on skid row with a flagon of port in a brown paper bag. (If you are buying your port in flagons, or purchasing your wine in a box you probably should have stopped drinking years ago, or at least converted to mineral water). But, the risk of unchecked alcoholism aside, a good beer, a fine wine and a quality spirit can be a stupendous party starter. There are so many wonderful ways to enjoy the social lubrication of a little tipple.

Wineries And Breweries

In recent years there has been a emerging trend for home brewing and boutique wineries and breweries, (we even have a boutique brewery in our street!). Many of these small operators offer unique products, like organic beer and wine, that you simply cannot get from a mainstream liquor stores. Many of these local breweries sell to local bars and pubs (this is very common in the UK), or open their doors directly to the public. Some have restaurants and cellar doors, and some even offer vineyard tours. There are many vineyards surrounding my city and it is possible to get a bus tour to take you from place to place to sample all the different wines. Many offer "clean skins", which are kind of like the lucky dip of the wine world. They are usually the end bottles from a production run, but what vintage and grape they are is often a mystery. They are often inexpensive to buy but could still be from a very high quality batch; or they could be like quaffing vinegar. It's quite an adventure!

Home Brewing

Craft beer is everywhere these days, and who doesn't love a pint? Home brewing is a great way to get your friends to come and visit. The mere mention of a boutique beer tasting is likely to see a stampede of willing Guinea Pigs (AKA taste testers) at your front door. With starter kits

WHAT TO DO IN *RETIREMENT*

beginning at about $100, home brewing can actually save you money. Of course in most places you are strictly forbidden from selling anything you brew, but there is nothing to stop you brewing up a batch for someone's birthday or for a Christmas present!

Oktoberfest

Break out the pretzels and lederhosen. Everyone should attend an Oktoberfest at least once in their lives. The undisputed king of beer festivals, Oktoberfest is legendary for it's oak barrels, busty serving wenches, oversized tankards and trombone wielding polka bands.

If you cannot get to Germany to enjoy the real deal don't worry; just about every city in the western world gives a nod to the occasion with their very own like named beer and vomit festival. Admittedly some of these copycat Oktoberfest's can be a little tragic, but you will still get to drink lots of beer.

WHAT TO DO IN *RETIREMENT*

15 SPORTY

OK, I am going to say this right up front. I am not a sporty person. While I love actively participating in some sports, I think I may have part of my brain missing when it comes to spectating. I genuinely don't understand why some people think the ability to kick a pig's bladder around a field of grass makes someone a hero, nor do I acknowledge that putting a ball in a hoop is something worth doing. And I certainly don't see why someone who is good at such a pointless task should be paid tens of millions of dollars to advertise shoes. I realise that I am in the minority on this and that my profound lack of understanding on these matters leaves me ill equipped to deal with this section of the book; that said, I know some people love sports and I am therefore prepared to have a go at it, but I suspect it won't be pretty.

Go Extreme

Break out the energy drinks and make like a twenty year old. If you like adrenal fatigue and the real possibility of ending up in traction there are plenty of extreme sporting options out there, including abseiling, skydiving, base-jumping, cave diving, wing-suit flying, kite-surfing, paragliding, paint ball, wind surfing and white water rafting. There is an extreme sport for just about every taste and sartorial preference. For example if you long to dress like a toddler but don't want to stand out among your piers skateboarding could be just the thing.

Maybe you like to look a little more formal? If you love the wild adventure of extreme sports but are worried you might be missing out on some of the more domestic joys, why not try extreme ironing?

According to Wikipedia: "Extreme ironing is both an extreme sport and a performance art in which people take ironing boards to remote locations and iron items of clothing".

According to the Extreme Ironing Bureau, extreme ironing is "the latest danger sport that combines the thrills of an extreme outdoor activity with the satisfaction of a well-pressed shirt."

Take A Hike

Up hill and down dale, walking is fresh air and nature, (or maybe diesel fumes and car horns if you happen to live on a motorway). But seriously, there are all kinds of walks. Whether you like to hike, dawdle, stride, stroll, saunter, sashay, meander, promenade, ramble, gallivant, traipse, tramp, or schlep around, there is a walk that is just right for you. Whether you are out to show off your sartorial best, or are clad in a parachute fabric sweat suit it doesn't matter.

Wherever you are, there are always fields, mountains, parks, beaches, esplanades and malls to be perambulated. Even if you're feeling a tad constitutionally disabled, shy of a wheelchair you can still get out for a good toddle hurple, limp or shuffle. And if you do happen to be in a wheel chair, then instead of walking you can just let the good times roll.

Lawn Bowls

Long known to be hotbeds of romance and intrigue you should never underestimate the radical nature of the lawn bowls crowd. Believe me, it's not all tea and cakes. While you may never have suspected it, within those starched white skirts and lovingly pressed trousers lurk some of the most outrageous flirts and party people on the planet. Lately some bowls clubs have even opened their doors to the rock and roll crowd. Understanding the truly radical nature of lawn bowlers these degenerate musicians and their entourages have flocked to join their ranks. If you are brave or out there enough to step into the fast lane then lawn bowls could be for you.

Ten-Pin Bowling

When you think about wearing shoes that have been on hundreds of feet before they got to you; when you consider the degenerative health effects of hot dogs, sodas and other bowling alley food; when your sole aim for the evening is to hurl heavy balls down long alleys in the hope of annihilating the

WHAT TO DO IN *RETIREMENT*

standing order, there is only one inescapable conclusion you can draw. Bowling is the every-man homage to entropy!

However, if you like creating chaos out of order, then you've got to love ten-pin bowling. Personally, I am drawn to anything that involves the catastrophic collision of fast moving balls and stationary objects. I love the sound of the pins crashing to the ground. I love the rise of the triumphant roar when someone scores a strike. I love the teams, the groovy 50's bowling shirts, the cancerous snack foods, it's all totally great. Of course, if you don't want your toes to mingle with the fungi of the masses, you could always buy your own shoes.

Croquet

Croquet may have been popular with the 'in' set back in the 1920's, when everyone was doing the Charleston and dressing like a flapper, but it's made a bit of comeback in recent times.

It's inexpensive, (you can pick up croquet set on EBay for $50-$100). It's gentle on the body, (so you don't need to have stellar strength, stamina or flexibility). You don't even need a manicured lawn. All you need is a rectangle of cut grass and some chalk (or string) to mark out your court. If you don't have the regulation 100 x 50 foot patch it doesn't matter, just adjust the size and shape of the court to fit the available space. For those that might want to get competitive there is even a US croquet association: "http://www.croquetamerica.com".

Take Aim At Archery

Archery is no longer a primitive hunting tool or medieval weapon of war, it is a thoroughly modern sport. It's not just for medievalists, or those that like to play cupid; it's perfect for anyone who enjoys rummaging through the woods searching for stray arrows. Whether you treat it as a hobby, get competitive, or would rather hunt down venison than visit your local butcher, archery is a tremendous; and unlike a lot of other sports, archers can rise to the top at any age. (American archer Galen Spencer won the gold in a Summer Olympics on his 64th birthday).

There are many different types of archery including traditional archery, target archery, field archery, 3D archery and bow hunting. Traditional archery is your free-range, "Hunger Games" kind of affair. Target archery is fairly self-explanatory; you simply set up a target and shoot arrows at it. Field archery is where you roam through the woods shooting at targets that have been set up along a track. 3D archery is similar to field archery but instead of shooting at targets you shoot at all kinds of foam model animals that have been skilfully hidden throughout the woods, and bow hunting is for those rugged outdoors types that like the visceral gore of killing one's own meat (seriously people, if you're not going to eat it, don't kill it).

Your choice of bow doesn't just depend on what kind of archery interests you and how strong you are. It is also about how cool you want to look while doing it. Compound bows are good all-rounders, they look impressive and are reasonably easy to use. Re-curve bows can look a bit geeky, but they are the easiest to handle and require the least physical strength. Long bows look very dramatic but require a lot of grunt, (seriously, it could destroy your shoulder trying to pull one of those things), whereas the crossbow is a hardcore hunting machine and could have you looking as menacing as Rambo on steroids.

Cue Up For Billiards

There are very few activities that are as equally welcomed in a refined English gentleman's club as they are in a Hell's angles hangout; but using long sticks to poke coloured balls around a felted slate table is one of them. The fact that cue sports are accepted by such a broad social spectrum makes them some of the most popular and widely played sports on the planet.

You don't need a body to rival Adonis, you don't even need to be fit; you just need a keen eye and a competitive spirit. If you don't own a table, you can enjoy the social aspect of playing in bars, pubs and clubs. It doesn't matter where you are in the world there will be some kind of pool or billiards competition being held within striking distance, and if you want to go semi pro the only equipment you'll need is a good cue stick.

Whether your game is carom, snooker, pool or billiards, the World Pool-Billiard Association (WPA), oversees a huge range of competitions and tournaments. They also have multi-national network of regional affiliates that spans the globe, including the All Africa Pool Association (AAPA), Asian Pocket Billiard Union (APBU), Billiard Congress of America (BCA, Canada

WHAT TO DO IN *RETIREMENT*

and the US), Confederation Panamerica of Billiards (CPB, Latin America and Caribbean), European Pocket Billiard Federation (EPBF, including Russia and the Near East), and last but not least the Oceania Pocket Billiard Association (OPBA, Australia, New Zealand, Pacific islands), so it shouldn't be too hard to find a trophy that's up for grabs somewhere close by.

The WPA and the World Confederation of Billiard Sports have been lobbying hard for cue sports to be included in the Olympics, which is looking increasingly likely. So who knows, if you practice hard enough you might even be able pocket an Olympic gold in your retirement.

Kick On With Martial Arts

While not a traditional pick for a quiet retirement, martial arts are surging in popularity with the over 50's, and not just because they provide a good workout. Martial arts can help you relax, clear the mind, and beat the living cr*p out of any wayward teen that tries a snatch and grab on your wallet.

Martial arts take many different forms, such as Jujitsu, Taekwondo, Karate, Tae-Bo, etc., so it's important that you find the martial art that is right for you. Some of your Bruce Lee, fly through the air kicking and screaming style martial arts can be pretty taxing on the body, but there a number of options that can be practiced to quite an advanced age. Chinese Kung Fu, (which includes forms like "Wing Chun" and "Shaolin Five Animal Style") and the modern Japanese practice of Akido, for example, are both great for older adults. Wing Chung focuses more on speed than raw power, and most of the striking is done open handed, (which is much gentler on the joints and muscles). Akido, which was developed early last century, is a synthesis of a range of martial arts, philosophical and religious beliefs. It was originally created so that practitioners could defend themselves while also protecting their attacker from injury.

Martial arts can be great for strength, cardio and mobility training. Of course, if your body is not used to exercise your muscles are going to get sore and some mild level of pain is to be expected, so take care not to exert yourself to the point of extreme pain. Unless of course you like that kind of thing?

Go Fly A Kite

Suggesting someone "Go fly a kite" may be a polite way to tell an extremely

WHAT TO DO IN *RETIREMENT*

annoying person to disappear, but it's also a mighty fine suggestion for anyone that needs to get out of the house. The first time I flew a kite I was amazed at just how physical and exhilarating it was. You really feel like you are one with the elements, weaving your kite through the wind, pulling, releasing, diving, flying, it's utterly brilliant. Kites can range in price from your simple child's $5 toy right through to professional $1000 models. You can even make your own. There is enormous amount of artistry and creativity on display in individually made kites. Birds, octopus, fish, kittens, insects, dragons, geometric shapes and colours all feature heavily in the kite maker's repertoire.

There is also a great community of kite fliers and festivals out there to explore. For those in the UK you can check out all the best kite festivals on the handy website www.kitecalendar.co.uk or if you are in the USA you might want to check out some of these kite fests. The Huntington Beach Kite Party or the Berkely kite festival in California, the Blossom Kite Festival in Washington DC, Kite Fest Louisiana, the Kids and Kites festival in Chicago, the Great lakes Kite Festival in Michigan, the Wild woods kite festival in New Jersey, the San Francisco kite festival, the summer or fall kite festival in Oregon, the Rogallo kite festival in Nth Carolina or the Washington State International Kite Festival. Wherever you happen to be there are plenty of fun kite festivals out there.

Go Fishing

OK, I get the solitude. I get the fresh air, the meditative, contemplative aspect, but the snaring a sharp hook though a fish's lip seems kind of barbaric. I'm sorry but I just cannot get past the notion that it would really hurt.

Fair enough if you are going to eat it and are prepared to kill it quickly and cleanly once you land it, but this notion of hooking a fish and throwing it back, or skewering live worms on hooks seems kind of like a training activity for psychopaths.

Body Building

If you feel a desperate need to parade around in skimpy Lycra then pumping a bit of iron first might not be a bad idea; after all bulging biceps are not just for twenty-somethings. There are a plethora of gyms, personal trainers,

WHAT TO DO IN *RETIREMENT*

trophy competitions and websites to help the mature age body builder achieve an insanely cut body. Contrary to what many people think, body-building is more than just strutting about flexing your muscles. It is a highly disciplined practice that tones up the mind as well as the body. It can improve your focus, determination, mental clarity and self-esteem, as well as your diet, muscle tone and bone density. Be careful though, if you get too strong it could put you on the favours list for any one in need of some heavy lifting.

On Your Bike

While biking can be perfect for greenies, fitness freaks and people without cars it is not without its risks. I don't want to be a Debbie downer here but if you are contemplating getting out on a bike in a city you need to know that biking can be fatal. Sad fact is that people on bicycles are often bullied and ignored by motorists. Cities with bike paths are usually fairly safe, but in most other places you could end up having a nice day out, or you could end up in traction! If you plan to stray off the bike paths I highly recommend you make your bike as visible as possible by covering it in those fluorescent flags and lighting it up like a Christmas tree! As for appropriate attire, helmets may make you look ridiculous and totally geeky, but they are a necessary evil. And while you don't need those spooky little Lycra shorts with padded bottom, you should wear something BRIGHT BRIGHT BRIGHT, like a high visibility vest or a fluorescent jumpsuit. If you still feel you need something brighter and more noticeable maybe you could entertain the children in passing cars by donning a clown suit? It would definitely make you more of a stand out!

Go Golfing

In this sport of millionaires, vast tracts of highly desirable land are set aside so that the fortunate few can play a rather extravagant form of "ball in a cup". Using long sticks with little wedges at the end golfers attempt to hit a small ball into a cup. The person who does it in the least hits is the winner.

To me golf seems like a long walk for people with short attention spans. You keep hitting the ball to remind yourself which way you are walking. But apparently you can remain competitive to quite an advanced age, which makes golf the perfect sport for mature people that still like to whip the youngsters.

WHAT TO DO IN *RETIREMENT*

Get On Target With Darts

Whether you want to get seriously competitive or just have bit of fun over a pint of larger, darts is one of the few sports that allows you to have a few drinks, shoot the breeze and practice all at the same time. Which isn't to say darts isn't a serious sport. The UK's PDC (professional darts corporation) hold a "World Championship" annually in the UK which has a prize fund of

£1,500,000, and the winner walks away with £300,000 (approximately US$400,000). Darts also has a good following in the USA.

The National Darts Association, ("www.ndarts.com"), have leagues all over North America, and they hold regular tournaments offering prizes of up to

$500,000. If you think you have a chance of hitting the bull's-eye, without taking someone's eye out, why not give it a shot?

Team Sports

Team sports are not for the feint hearted. If you mess up in a solo sport you only have to deal with your own disappointment. Stuff up in a team sport and you have let the entire side down. Conversely, if you win no one cheers for you personally, they cheer for the team. So you get only, maybe, one tenth of the glory you would on a solo endeavor. It's simple math really. Playing team sports = 10 x the potential down side with only 1/10th of the potential upside. Yes, I know some people love playing basketball, baseball, netball, cricket, soccer, football, polo, hockey, lacrosse and volleyball etc., for the wonderful camaraderie etc., but trust me, with team sports most of the time you only one fumble away from exile!

Target And Clay Shooting

Shooting is another sport where you can remain competitive throughout your life. Senior target shooters are consistently making their way onto the Olympic podium. So if you are going to shoot anything target shooting is definitely the way to go. Targets don't feel it when you pop off a riffle round, or unload a clip into them. And if you want something a bit more challenging clay ducks provide excellent moving targets. Fun with guns, and no one gets hurt! What could be better than that?

Anyone For Tennis?

WHAT TO DO IN *RETIREMENT*

Never mind the sporty moustaches of the club coaches, the little white player's outfits, or its extraordinary popularity, tennis is the only game in the world where being a total loser gets you love! This fact alone clearly makes tennis one of the best sports ever invented. Animal activists need not be put off either. It's been a very long time since tennis rackets have been strung with catgut, so tennis is now totally Vegan friendly.

16 LUCRATIVE

Supplement Your Income

While some people love working part-time after they retire, others are forced into it by necessity. But whatever the reason, a small business activity can be a great way to earn a bit extra cash. Everyone knows it can be a bit of a grind trying to carve out a few extra bucks but some methods are easier, and considerably more fun than others.

Have A Yard Sale

Yard sales are a great way to get rid of junk while communing with others in your neighbourhood. You never know who will turn up. When I was younger my mother used to love having yard sales. She loved it so much that she would scour the local trash and treasure markets and car boot sales just to have something to sell. She made some great friendships and she made a pretty penny at it too!

Become A Gold Digger

Marry someone rich for his or her money! Well maybe it's not your first choice in retirement planning but that doesn't mean you have to give up on your gold digging dream; after all, there could be gold in them there hills! Are you in an area where they once found gold? Grab a metal detector and take it for a walk. Old safety pins, tin cans, an old stirrup, there's no telling what you might find.

Airbnb

Air BnB is a website that turns ordinary people's houses into makeshift bed and breakfast accommodation. If you love "meeting new people" Air BnB is not only a wonderful way to have a nose around inside other people's places

WHAT TO DO IN *RETIREMENT*

when you're travelling, but it's a great way to get totally unknown strangers into your home to stay with you.

It's not totally random though, as the website does have a rating system for guests and hosts to rate and reviews their experiences. However, if you just want the money and don't want to interact with a steady stream of random strangers you could have a section of your home converted into a miniature hotel suite, with a private bathroom and cooking facilities, (although realistically if you can afford to do that you probably don't need the money).

Sell Your Opinion

Why not do online surveys?... OK, this really is as dull as watching paint dry, but it requires no real thought or skill and can rake in a small amount of cash. Some online surveys don't pay participants with actual money. Instead companies offer discounts and even free products to people who are willing to give up a little time to answer some questions If you are keen to give online surveys a go then I recommend giving wildly inappropriate answers to spice up this rather dull activity. The wilder and more outrageous the answers the more fun it could be.

Build A Website

WHAT TO DO IN *RETIREMENT*

We now live in an age of shameless self-promotion and there is no reason you can't be a part of that. Nothing screams "look at me" louder than owning the URL (web address) to your own name, and having a multi page web site to serve as a testament to your limitless brilliance.

www.wix.com is a great place to start for those that have no experience in the dark art of web site construction, although you could save money by starting a site on www.wordpress.com for free (there are plenty of videos on how to do it on Youtube).

But seriously, not all web sites are shameless self-promotion. You can advertise anything, including a charity or an NGO.

Sell Your Handicrafts

While you might enjoy knitting or making clothes and can create things that others would be happy to pay for, the reality is that selling your own handicrafts is a great way to ensure you are paid at the same hourly rate as a third world factory worker. In this age of mass production no one really wants to pay for hand crafted artefacts, so do not, repeat DO NOT do this just for the money. (The only exceptions to this rule are for those marketing geniuses whom are simply brilliant at branding, and mythologising their own work). While you can technically sell your crafts online, or go to local flea markets to display your wares, this is something you should do primarily for FUN FUN FUN (and pocket change). It's true that if your crafts become popular enough, you might find that people will track you down just to buy them (and pay you a good price), but don't go in expecting that. My advice, keep it weird, quirky and above all FUN!

Become An EBay Star

EBay is an excellent way to supplement an income, or just clear out the junk you no longer want. You can sell just about ANYTHING on EBay. As a bet I framed a brown paper bag, and titled it "Concept Art - Brown Paper Bag", and sold it for $35. Admittedly it took a few weeks but it did sell, so the principal is solid. There are lots of other websites, like Craig's List or Gumtree, where you can buy and sell, and the ads are free!

Get A Part-Time Job

This is not serious advice unless you are forced into it by circumstance. The

WHAT TO DO IN *RETIREMENT*

whole point of retirement is that no one is telling you what to do anymore. I know some people like to work, although to my mind getting a part time job defeats the purpose of retirement. If you want a part time job for social interaction or because you just love your work, then OK. But make sure it's on your terms!

Write An E-book And Sell It On Amazon

The fact that you are reading this book right now should provide you with ample evidence that this can be done by someone of limited literary skill, questionable humour and a rather modest intelligence. This alone should be enough to inspire you. There are a few tips and tricks to doing it well, but nothing doctor Google couldn't dig up for you. If you need formatting done "www.upwork.com" is the place. If you want a cheap cover put together try "www.fiverr.com" or "www.upwork.com"

Sell From Your Garden

If you are an avid gardener you could turn your talent into a small business? From fruit and vegetables to eggs, compost and cuttings, there is a huge range of stuff from the garden that you can sell or swap. People are always looking to buy quality plants and produce that are free from industrial chemicals and pesticides. One of my neighbours propagates succulents and sells them from her front porch every weekend. Another man I know has turned his garden into nursery. They both do quite well. I have even heard rumours that there are certain herbs that can be sold for staggeringly large amounts of money, but as yet no one has offered me a princely sum for my basil. Go figure?

Play The Stock Market

Playing the stock market is fun, and can be very profitable but it is really just legitimate gambling; so definitely don't do it with any money you cannot afford to lose. (This is actually good advice!) While the odds are decidedly better than at the casino there are real risks; by all means play but don't bet the farm.

Become A Landlord

If you don't have enough headaches in your life you could try buying some cheap rental property in a questionable neighbourhood and renting it out to drug addicts. This is one of the best ways I know of to add a level of tension and unpredictability to your life without actually leaving the house or doing

WHAT TO DO IN *RETIREMENT*

anything physically dangerous. (Although banging on the door demanding the rent could lead to trouble). If you want to try this exciting pastime make sure you have good insurance.

17 SPIRITUAL

Explore Your Spiritual Side

Throughout the Ages countless parables, myths and stories have been manufactured to explain the inexplicable and imbue our lives with a sense of purpose. Of course, these stories may or may not be true, but what ever "the truth" actually is we still like to think there is something bigger out there than our personal peep-hole into the universe. Musing on what that might be, and which spiritual franchise, if any, has the patent on the real deal is a superb way to fill your days.

Explore The Religions Of The World

Comparative religion is an excellent interest for religious zealots, casual believers, aggressive secularists and the just plain curious. Everyone can get something out of studying the faiths of the world.

Is there a correct religion, and if there is how do you know you were born into it? Maybe there is wisdom in other faiths that would resonate with you. Do you know which major world religions does not believe in god? What exactly do Islam, Christianity and Judaism have in common? Is there any crossover between Hinduism and Buddhism? Why are the Janes extreme pacifists? Why do Sufis like to whirl? How would you know the answer to these questions if you never looked into it? Countless millions have fought and died in the name of their religion, so it's kind of interesting to study what it is that they saw as worth dying for.

Join A Religious Group

If you are totally convinced that your religion is the correct one, or even if you just like a bit of company, why not join a religious congregation.

WHAT TO DO IN *RETIREMENT*

Attending regular religious gatherings is a great way to experience your human connectedness, and possibly avoid eternal damnation in the process.

While there are many fine religious groups that do a lot of selfless community work these groups are by no means your only options. If you simply want to belong to a like-minded community, shun other groups, foster your sense of moral superiority and enjoy the odd bake sale, there are plenty of religious groups out there that will cater to your needs. If however you are joining a religious group in order to avoid eternal damnation you may ultimately be disappointed, because apparently you have to pick the right denomination of the right religion so God won't be really upset with you. Given how many different brands there are out there your chances of picking the right one are really no better than lottery odds.

Master Meditation

Contrary to conservative opinion meditation is not all navel gazing and OMMing. There are hundreds of different meditation techniques out there, and there is bound to be one that suits you. Did you know the Catholic rosary is a form of meditation? Meditation is like a gymnasium for the mind. It tones up your ability to focus, increases awareness, relaxes the body and generally helps one become more resilient. There are yuppie organisations like TM where you can pay thousands to learn their special brand, or there are free courses provided by some secular groups. There are also many free meditation courses run by Buddhist and Hindu groups.

Flex Out With Yoga

If you didn't get your fill of free love and radical eastern philosophies in the 60's and 70's, you will be thrilled to know that yoga is now totally mainstream. You can now bend and stretch to your hearts content and no-one will accuse you of subverting the dominant cultural paradigm. Apparently yoga can make you stronger and suppler, which can lead to better sex (or so I am told), but please don't let that put you off. If you are not into the whole tantric thing yoga can also provide some excellent rationales for getting all pious and puritanical.

Centre Yourself With Tai Chi

In the west we tend to think of tai chi as being an extremely slow form of oriental exercise, but according to Wikipedia the term "t'ai chi ch'uan" translates as "supreme ultimate fist", "boundless fist", "supreme ultimate boxing" or "great extremes boxing", which all sounds frighteningly macho.

In reality tai chi is more like a martial art, a meditation, and an exercise regime all rolled into one; so while it may give you fists that could single- handedly take out an army of street thugs, hopefully it also gives you the self- control not to use them.

The health benefits of tai chi have been praised by thousands of daily practitioners, so why not head to the park for a dawn class?

Commune With Nature

Tree hugging, nudism, mud rolling, skinny-dipping, ice diving, there are so many ways to get in touch with the natural world. You don't need to move to the county; simply walk in the park, plant a tree or go to the water's edge and breathe! Nature is you friend, so don't be a stranger.

18 CHARITABLE

Volunteer

I am not suggesting volunteering for the French foreign legion, or as a human guinea pig for some sinister medical experimentation. I am talking about social service. Working at homeless shelters, mentoring needy kids, or just generally helping people in your community. There are so many ways to make a difference. You can visit the elderly in hospital or tutor at your local school. Some volunteer work is very social. For example many cities have programs where volunteers help tourists navigate their city. In Auckland, New Zealand there is even a lively group of volunteers that make free cups of tea for people in the arrivals hall at the airport. There is so much joy to be had in helping others, so why not grab a piece of that happiness?

Become A Foster Carer

It is a sad reality that even in first world countries there are a lot of children not getting the love, care and stability they need. There is a desperate need for people who can provide foster care to step in and fill the gap for these kids. If you have a safe home, energy and love to spare this could be an amazing gift to someone in need. My sister had a foster child live with her and her daughter for a couple of years and it was a great experience for my niece, (who is an only child). Most jurisdictions offer some level of financial support for carers who take in needy children, so even you are not flush it may still be an option.

Help Out With Animal Rescue

Becoming an animal rescuer is a wonderfully rewarding thing to do. Whether you take in injured wildlife or needy domestic animals, the love and care you give can literally save lives. If you cannot take on a pet full time there are

WHAT TO DO IN *RETIREMENT*

many charities and services that will provide you with food and veterinary care while they either search for a permanent home for the animal, or rehabilitate it for re-release back into the wild. This can be a tremendous way for someone who is unable to take on a pet for life to get the joy and benefits of caring for another living creature.

Feed The Homeless

You can volunteer at a shelter or registered charity, or you can just go out and do it. You will be pleased to know that some of the proceeds of this book go to feed the homeless. But I must confess, I don't do this just because I am a lovely person (which of course, I am). It's actually a totally selfish act! Feeding homeless people is one of the most amazingly feel good things I have ever done. I fill my shopping trolley with sandwiches, fruit and bottled water and head off into the city. My husband and I walk the streets offering food and drink to any homeless people we see. For the $40 it takes to stock the cart, I can get far more joy, satisfaction and purpose that any cinema, show or fancy restaurant meal has ever bought me.

For anyone who is scared by this concept, please don't be. In my experience most homeless people have suffered some kind of trauma or misfortune, which has lead to job loss, addiction, and in some cases depression or mental illness; but the smiles that come to suffering people's faces when you stop and talk to them, ask them their stories, and show them some kindness, are some of the deepest, most profound smiles I have ever seen. If you have never done this, then I highly recommend it. It can put your life squarely into perspective.

Hold A Charity Gala

If you like your social work with a little more celebrity glam, why not try high-end fundraising. There are plenty of rich folk out there who would never get their hands dirty at the coalface of social service, but would happily spend thousands on a plate at a charity gala.

Learn To Love Other People

OK, we are not talking about the "swinging" kind of love here, (although if you really want to and your partner is up for it then more power to you); we are talking agape, fraternity, sorority and love for our fellow humans. Everyone knows that humanity can be pretty dreadful. There are so many annoying, selfish, stupid people out there. That's why loving humanity is such a great challenge to take on. It's like climbing Everest. There are so many obstacles to overcome, but once you get there you will be on top of the world.

The fact is, tolerance, compassion, empathy, kindness, generosity and patience serve their possessor far more than their recipient, so why not give it a go? Even if you still have well founded doubts and suspicions about other people, you can still learn to love them and treat them with kindness.

WHAT TO DO IN *RETIREMENT*

19 NOMADIC

Hit The Road

Let the spirit of Willie Nelson wash over you. The anonymity, the appallingly bad gas station food, the curious cast of characters that pop up along the way; road trips are a magical kind of freedom. They even have their own movie genre. Whether you have a caravan or camper, or just a car, everyone knows roads are simply begging to be hit, and who better to hit them than you?

Take A Day Trip

Admittedly taking a trip doesn't mean quite what it did in the 60's and 70's, but that doesn't mean it can't still be fun. Unless you live in Antarctica or the wilds of Siberia there is probably something totally fabulous within a days drive of where you are now.

Caravans And RV's

If you love clogging up traffic on small country roads and staying in trailer parks, McDonald's car parks and friend's driveways, then caravans and RV's are definitely for you!

There is a level of comfort and predictability to traveling with your own hotel room in tow. You can potter at your own pace, or join convoy with other RV enthusiasts. Why not take a caravan to Burning Man or Glastonbury? Go on a spiritual pilgrimage to see all the "LARGE" things. (I am particularly keen to see the world's largest shrimp.)

Guided Tours

Whether it is one of those tourist buses that circles most cities, a walking tour of the local sites, a bus ride past the houses of celebrities or a guided tour

WHAT TO DO IN *RETIREMENT*

through a gallery, winery, museum, historical village, or even a film studio, short day tours are everywhere. They are usually easy on the pocket, not too taxing on the schedule and are a fantastic way to explore wherever you happen to be. Usually the guides are a wealth of intriguing information that you just wouldn't get if you simply poked around on your own.

Take A Cruise

If you love Hawaiian shirts, straw hats, chlorine pools, playing quoites, nerdy bands and endless smorgasbords full of average cold cuts, then cruising is definitely for you. On the downside, if there are any fellow cruisers that are so excruciatingly boring that they make you want to jump overboard, you will be stuck with them for the duration. Don't be overly discouraged though, even with the most persistently annoying of co-passengers you should still be able to find a spot on deck where you can enjoy the solitude of staring silently out across the crystal waters, (at the very you least you should be able to lose them when you are in port).

Join The Jet Set

Air travel has never been cheaper. These days you can get just about anywhere without breaking the bank. And there are all kinds of weird and wonderful deals from the airlines; like around the world tickets, where you can have a set number of stops but you have to keep flying in the same direction. Then there is the much loved mystery flight, where you book a return flight at the airport and they put you on the first seat that comes up regardless of where it is going. But commercial airlines are far from the only way to fly. You could book a jaunt in a charter plane, a glider, a helicopter or even a seaplane.

Package Tours

If you always hated colouring outside the lines a package tour might be just right for you. If you love the security and comfort of travelling with a group, having a well-defined budget and a predetermined itinerary and activity schedule, a package tour can take all the worry out of planning your trip. A good travel package should include your transportation, guided tour groups, and accommodation and breakfasts. While you can always make friends with other people on the same package, you could also get your own group together.

WHAT TO DO IN *RETIREMENT*

Up Up And Away

Hot air ballooning is an extraordinary experience. It's not just the sense of being so high up in an open basket, it's the sound of the wind, the absence of the engine, and of course it is all about the champagne and strawberries as you float across the skies.

Explore Your Own Backyard

Why not try being a tourist in your town or city? Pull on those travel slacks; sling your camera around your neck and step outside your own front door. Many people live in a place their whole lives without ever realizing all of the magic that is right under their noses.

It's human nature to take things that are at hand for granted, but in so doing you can miss out on the fun and adventure that is right there for the taking. If you are really scratching for a local destination try checking out the local tourist bureau. They will have a wealth of information about what's on offer; and will probably be able to point you to amazing things that you never knew were there.

See The World!

Everyone knows that their country is the best and every other country in the world is doing it wrong. The fact is, other countries just don't understand how things ought to be done and clearly they need people to go over there and set them straight. Missionaries and world travellers have been doing this for centuries, so why not join them?

Be amazed by how people from other lands have no understanding or sympathy for your special brand of culture. Vent your anger at locals who don't understand you when you speak slowly and loudly at them in your own language. Offend countless people by having no understanding of what is acceptable in their culture.

But seriously, world travel is an excellent way to broaden your horizons, and step outside your own culture. Experience things from a different perspective, like the view from on top of an elephant, or the giddy heights of Machu Picchu. Take a trip on the Orient Express, wander the Silk Road, ride a camel across the desert. Apart from the all unfamiliar sights, sounds and smells there is a world full of people out there just ready to make new friends.

WHAT TO DO IN *RETIREMENT*

You can find special travel packages that will take you from the east to the west, and the north to the south. There really are no limits to where you can go, so why not see it all?

20 THE LIFE AQUATIC

Since the dawn of time humanity has had a fascination with water. Most of the world's surface is water. Most of our bodies are made up of water. Without water we simply could not survive. Since before recorded history we have been taking to the sea for food, for travel and for the sheer pleasure of it, so get out there.

Snorkelling

This is a great pastime for those that prefer to swim with the fish rather than catch them. Apparently there are over three million shipwrecks on the ocean floor, not to mention some extraordinary coral reefs. While snorkelling can be done in the shallows for next to nothing, deep sea diving is not a cheap exercise. However, if you don't mind the possibility of coming nose to nose with a shark, or breathing tank air then this activity could be for you.

Deep sea diving requires a lot of expensive equipment and it all needs to be kept in top order, so it is probably better to take some classes to see if it is really for you before you splash out on a kit. There are many diving schools held in local swimming pools where you can learn the basic diving skills without spending a fortune or risking life and limb. That said, deep sea diving has a reputation for being one of the most incredible experiences there is. What better way to while away the days than to get your wetsuit on and explore the ocean floor.

Boating

Once the purview of the mega rich, anyone of modest means can now enjoy a day on the water. Admittedly it might be in a tiny little dinghy or a rusty old sail boat, but a day on the water is a day on the water. If you are really desperate to get out there you could even catch a ferry. Many cities and towns

WHAT TO DO IN *RETIREMENT*

have modestly priced ferries as part of their public transport system. What better way to see New York from the water on a shoestring?

Get In The Swim

Swimming is so much more than a great way to cool down on a hot day. Whether you go jump in the lake, dive into a swimming pool, hit the waves at the beach, or splash out in a dam or river, swimming is a great stress reliever. It is also one of the best exercises for anyone over 40. It builds endurance, increases cardiovascular fitness, tones your muscles, builds strength and helps in maintaining a healthy body weight; all while taking the impact stress off your body. Swimming is pretty well everything you could want in workout. It's the perfect exercise for anyone with any kind of muscular skeletal problem arthritis, bad back or asthma.

Dive Right In

If you live near a swim centre with a diving pool then you are in luck. High diving is quite possibly the most thrilling, most exhilarating experiences you can have for pocket change. Most pools will let you dive over and over again for the price of a single entry ticket. The best thing is, diving is really very low risk, especially for something that can give you such a surge of adrenalin. Even if you are not quite up to jumping off the high tower, you can still get quite a rush hurling yourself off the lower levels.

Water Polo

If you enjoy all the health benefits of swimming, but would prefer something a bit more competitive and social, why not check and see if your local swimming centre has a water polo team that is suitable for you. If they don't, and the idea appeals, why not start one?

Workout In The Water

Aquarobics classes are the perfect place to show off your skirted swimsuit and floral bathing cap. Yes, there will be some annoyingly over enthusiastic 20 year old with a ghetto blaster bouncing up and down poolside, yelling at you to move it, but you can ignore her.

It's the perfect exercise for those with a little more girth or those that simply prefer to float through their exercises. Chances are you will find water aerobics classes at your local swimming pool.

WHAT TO DO IN *RETIREMENT*

Paddle Your Own Canoe

The combined forces of evolution and human ingenuity have been hard at work on the hollow log. So much so that these days there are a whole range of floating, paddling sports to indulge in. Whether you fancy the relative solitude of canoeing and kayaking, the highly honed team co-ordination of a six person rowing team, or just paddling round the lake in a giant floating bicycle, it's a great way to get fit and enjoy the sunshine of the day. Of course, if you prefer to sit back and let someone else do all the hard work for you, a trip to Venice for a ride in a gondola might be in order.

21 TECHNICAL

I realise that most people already know their way around a computer, and if you are reading this as an e-book you could probably just skip ahead now. But if you are a committed Luddite now is the time to seriously get over it.

Get Online

No matter what you are interested in the Internet will help you do it faster, cheaper and better. And it's not just the boring mundane stuff like doing your banking, paying your bills and ordering your grocery shop. You can get in touch with others who share your interests, find cheap hotels, cheap airfares, bargain wines, art supplies, obscure music and literature, the latest advances in kayaks, gardening tips, special interest clubs, online dating, in fact you can find just about anything you can think of on the net. I even found a husband!

Refusing to use a computer is like refusing to learn to read. Sure you can have a life without reading, but that life is not going to be as rich, and everything you do is going to be far more difficult. If you cannot find someone in your sphere who can help you get on line then most towns have some kind of free classes available, so check with your local library, council or shire for what is available in your area.

Write An App. Or A Computer Program

Apparently it is not that hard to do. The Internet is full of instructions and programs to help you do it. It could be a game, a recipe builder, a scrapbook maker, a heart rate monitor, an app. that orders your breakfast at the local cafe, or even an app. to tell you when a Mormon missionary is approaching your door so you can get the tea and cakes ready; it could be anything at all.

Build A Robot Or An Electronic Gizwaz

WHAT TO DO IN *RETIREMENT*

You can get all kinds of kits from your local electronics store, or design your own. There are countless electronic projects you can throw together. Contrary to what you may think amateur electronics is not just for 15 year-olds. I know a man who actually retired on the proceeds of a foot pedal he designed. You can build your own doorbell, graphic equalizer, synthesizer, maybe even a robot slave to do your bidding?

22 FAMILY ORIENTED

I admit that this may or may not be a bonus depending on the nature of your family. If your family is populated by violent, anti social criminals you might want to give it a miss, but if your family is all warm fuzzy bear hugs and endless camp fire sing-alongs then by all means enjoy.

See More Of Your Siblings

No one understands the unique madness you had to endure growing up better than your siblings. No one will ever get your jokes, quirks and idiosyncrasies quite like they do. They have known you throughout the best and the worst of your life. They know the setbacks you have suffered, and the victories you have won. Unfortunately, sometimes the pressures of your own family, the tyranny of distance, or even long unresolved conflict can lead to us losing touch with our brothers and sisters. Now is the time to reconnect. While it may not always work out the way we want it to, reconnecting with long lost, or rarely seen family is always worth a try. You could be pleasantly surprised.

Hang Out With Your Grand-kids

Do you enjoy visits from your grandchildren, or are they a bit whiny and demanding? The next time your kids dump their kids on you why not get your own back by teaching the little darlings the finer points of mud pie making, finger painting, clay modelling or anything else that will get them totally caked in muck for the car ride home. Give them a festival of filth and they will just love coming to see you!

Of course if they are a bit more computer game oriented why not join them in wasting their lives. Online worlds like "World of Warcraft" for example can eat up years of valuable time you could otherwise spend actually living.

WHAT TO DO IN *RETIREMENT*

Genealogy And Ancestry

No need to limit your family interaction just to the currently living. Why not have a nose around the family tree? Who knows, go back far enough and your sleuthing may turn up some unexpected royalty, some toffee nosed aristocracy or maybe even a coal miner. Ancestry can get quite addictive, so it's good to know that you don't have to restrict yourself to your immediate family. If get the bug there is nothing to stop you tracking back the ancestral lines of your friend's families, your siblings or children's partners, or even the deep dark family past of a favourite celebrity.

23 A Quick Word In Closing

The world is full of strange and wonderful octopus, bats, spiders, frogs, gnats, elephants, ant eaters, mosquitoes, chickens, pheasants, turkeys, donkeys, horses, zebras, dogs, wolves, tree ferns, daisies, periwinkles, mice, impala, ladybugs, flies, moths, shrews, moles, slow worms, snakes, eels, sharks, whales, dolphins, fish, corals, muscles, clams, crocodiles, alligators etc., and somehow you managed to be lucky enough to be born human.

Blessed with a critical thinking brain, opposable thumbs and an endless range of possibilities we humans should not squander the great gift we have been given.

Life is short, and may or may not have any meaning beyond the meaning we give it. The one thing we can do to truly honour this life is to live it to the fullest for as many days as we are able.

Be as kind and patient as you can be with others. Be relentless in your quest for a fully actualized life! Enjoy the freedoms you have, for they are but the blink of an eye.

Seize your day, and laugh heartily! Cheers Stella

Resources

There are literally countless resources out there, many of them totally free. It is the joy of the digital age that you can learn just about anything, find just about anyone or go just about anywhere, and do it all more cheaply and easily than at any other time in human history.

You can use websites like www.meetup.com to find people, groups or clubs in your local area that share you interests, or you could take up a FREE online course. While I have barely scratched the surface of what is available I want to offer you this list of FREE (well most of them should be) courses and resources. This list is by no means comprehensive, but it should give you some idea of the breadth and scope what is out there and available to anyone with access to a computer.

General Academic Courses

www.edx.org

http://www.openculture.com/freeonlinecourses http://oedb.org/open/

www.coursera.org www.extension.harvard.edu/open-learning-initiative
General Writing Courses

https://www.class-central.com/report/writing-free-online-courses/
http://www.creative-writing-now.com/free-online-writing-courses.html
http://bubblecow.com/free-online-writing-courses   http://bit.ly/29mbTg8

www.futurelearn.com/courses/start-writing- fiction

General Music Courses

WHAT TO DO IN *RETIREMENT*

www.edx.org/school/berkleex

www.springboard.com/blog/30-best-free-online-music-courses/
http://www.berkleeshares.com/

http://www.earmaster.com/music-theory-online/course-introduction. html
https://alison.com/learn/music

http://www.open.edu/openlearn/history-the-arts/culture/music
http://study.com/articles/10_Sources_for_Free_Online_Music_Courses.html

Piano Courses

http://www.pianonanny.com/ https://www.hoffmanacademy.com/
http://www.zebrakeys.com/

https://www.youtube.com/watch?v=ggIDo2Fsv48
http://www.gopiano.com/ http://www.learnpianoonline.com/

http://www.true-piano-lessons.com/free-piano-lessons.html

Guitar Courses

http://www.guitarlessons.com/guitar-lessons/ http://www.justinguitar.com/
https://www.guitartricks.com/ http://www.theguitarsuite.com/
http://guitarcompass.com/free-lessons/ http://www.tabs4acoustic.com/en/

Screenwriting Courses and Resources

http://www.bbc.co.uk/writersroom/opportunities/introduction-to-

Screenwriting

http://www.my ik.com/FilmSchool/screenwriting.html https://www.lights lmschool.com/blog/free-screenwriting-courses/
http://www.scriptmag.com/free/

http://www.filminquiry.com/10-mostly-free-online-courses- filmmaking/

Journalism Courses

WHAT TO DO IN RETIREMENT

http://study.com/articles/List_of_Free_Online_Journalism_Classes_and_Courses.html http://www.mulinblog.com/mulinblog-online-j-school-course-schedule/ http://www.onlinecollege.org/2009/05/20/skip-journalism-school-50- free-open-courses/ http://journalismdegree.org/2009/top-50-free-open-courseware-classes- for-journalists/

Photography Courses

https://www.creativelive.com/photography
https://www.udemy.com/draft/23338/
http://petapixel.com/2014/07/03/best-free-online-photography- courses-tutorials/ http://freephotocourse.com/online-photography-course.html http://digitalphotobuzz.com/6-totally-free-online-photography-classes

Gardening Courses

http://www.openlearningworld.com/innerpages/Vegetable%20Gardening.htm

https://www.greenwoodnursery.com/free-online-gardening-courses
http://www.organicauthority.com/organic-gardening/top-5-online-gardening- courses.html

http://www.freestudentcourses.co.uk/gardening/
http://www.bbc.co.uk/learning/subjects/gardening.shtml

Stained Glass Courses

https://www.youtube.com/watch?v=EZL1ktDPt0g
https://www.youtube.com/watch?v=E0xACBQa4UQ&list=PLEA6731D93C734AB2

Carpentry Courses

http://study.com/articles/List_of_Free_Online_Carpentry_Courses_Classes_and_Learning_Materials.html http://www.thewoodwhisperer.com/

ABOUT THE AUTHOR

The world is full of strange and wonderful octopus, bats, spiders, frogs, gnats, elephants, ant eaters, mosquitoes, chickens, pheasants, turkeys, donkeys, horses, zebras, dogs, wolves, tree ferns, daisies, periwinkles, mice, impala, ladybugs, flies, moths, shrews, moles, slow worms, snakes, eels, sharks, whales, dolphins, fish, corals, muscles, clams, crocodiles, alligators etc., and somehow you managed to be lucky enough to be born human.

Blessed with a critical thinking brain, opposable thumbs and an endless range of possibilities we humans should not squander the great gift we have been given.

Life is short, and may or may not have any meaning beyond the meaning we give it. The one thing we can do to truly honour this life is to live it to the fullest for as many days as we are able.

Be as kind and patient as you can be with others. Be relentless in your quest for a fully actualized life! Enjoy the freedoms you have, for they are but the blink of an eye.

Seize your day, and laugh heartily! Cheers

Made in the USA
San Bernardino, CA
20 June 2020